Hear the Bugles Calling

HEAR THE BUGLES CALLING

My Three Wars as a Combat Infantryman

LIONEL F. PINN, SR.
WITH FRANK SIKORA

NewSouth Books
Montgomery | Louisville

NewSouth Books
P.O. Box 1588
Montgomery, AL 36102

Copyright © 2007 by Frank Sikora and Wenonah Pinn Resha.
All rights reserved under International and Pan-American Copyright Conventions.
Originally published in 2001 with the ISBN 1-58838-060-2 by Court Street Press, a division of NewSouth, Inc., Montgomery, Alabama.

Library of Congress Cataloging-in-publication data
Pinn, Lionel F. (Lionel Francis), 1923-1999
Hear the bugles calling : my three wars as a combat infantryman / Lionel F. Pinn, Sr. with Frank Sikora.
p. cm.
ISBN-13: 978-1-60306-025-7
ISBN-10: 1-60306-025-1
1. Pinn, Lionel F. (Lionel Francis), 1923-1999. 2. United States. Army—Non-commissioned officers—Biography. 3. United States. Army. Infantry—Biography. 4. World War, 1939-1945—Personal narratives, American. 5. Korean War, 1950-1953—Personal narratives, American. 6. Vietnamese Conflict, 1961-1975—Personal narratives, American. I. Sikora, Frank, 1936- II. Title.
U53.P47 A3 2001
355'.0092—dc21
[B]
2001055255

Second Edition, 2007

Design by Randall Williams
Printed in the United States of America

TO ALL MY FAMILY AND FRIENDS

AND

TO THOSE WHO SERVED

Contents

Foreword 9
Prologue 15

PART ONE: WORLD WAR II

1 Born To Be a Warrior 20
2 Entering the Army 23
3 Pearl 31
4 Combat: New Guinea 36
5 Fighting in the Islands 55
6 Army Rust 62

PART TWO: KOREA

7 A Soldier Again 68
8 A New Love and a New War 73
9 On the Naktong 76
10 Snow . . . and Chinese Everywhere 88
11 Chinese Capture and Escape 99
12 Leaving Korea 110

PART THREE: LAOS & VIETNAM

13 Fort Benning 132
14 "Listen to the Rice Grow" 134
15 Prelude to Vietnam 138
16 Home Fires in Nam Tha 143
17 Delivering Babies for the Laotians 146

Eight pages of photographs begin on page 123.

18	River Doctor	150
19	An Uncertain Peace	161
20	Back to the States	163
21	Training Cubans	165
22	The Reason Una Left	167
23	Vietnam	170
24	In a Spirit World	178
25	Last Call: 1968–1969	184
26	The World from House 10	195

PART FOUR: RETREAT

27	Retirement and Judy	200
28	Action in Grenada	205
29	Return to Laos	209
30	Old Soldiers, All	215

After-Battle Report   220

Foreword

ALL MEN — AND WOMEN — who have been in combat share a common life thread that the rest of us never know. While all those who served — whether on the ground, at sea, or in the air — faced the prospect of capture, injury, or death, it is generally conceded that the infantry soldier probably drew the worst duty. Not only was he being shot at, but he endured the misery of hot jungles or paralyzing cold. His life was on the line not day by day, but almost minute by minute.

In 1995, I met such a man in Guntersville, Alabama. Lionel F. Pinn was an American Indian, and even though he was 72 at the time, he was in great shape, erect, with broad shoulders. The purpose of the meeting was a newspaper interview about his military career, which spanned three wars — all as a front-line infantry soldier. What he told me that day was fascinating. The man had escaped death countless times. "The Good Lord wasn't ready for me yet," he explained.

He pointed to the miniature Combat Infantryman Badge he wore on his green blazer. The badge bore two silver stars, meaning he had earned it three times, a rarity. "This is what I'm most proud of," he said. "The other medals don't mean that much."

Pinn, who'd spent 30 years in the Army, was then working as the chief jailer at the Marshall County Jail. Men like Lionel never retire.

I kept in touch with him and we later decided to put his memories of World War II, Korea, and Vietnam, into a book. We met a dozen times or more, spending hours trying to structure his memories into a cohesive time frame. The interviews took much of 1996. Then in March 1997, doctors at University Hospital in Birmingham found that Lionel had leukemia. I visited him the day the diagnosis was confirmed. "They say I'll be lucky if I live a year," he confided. "Isn't that something? Survive three damn wars then get something like this."

The interviews became less frequent then, and work slowed. The dozens of questions I had would never be answered. Lionel died in August 1999. Yet I kept working on his story so that it could be published and others could know of his achievements and courage. The voice that you hear in this book, from the Prologue on, is his. I helped structure the book, but it is told in Lionel's own words.

When we worked on this project, Lionel insisted that it not be overly long, and that it be aimed at the average reader and not necessarily the military professional. We avoided much of the technical aspects of warfare, such as the numerous acronyms and descriptions of military hardware.

Many helped in the effort to bring this book together. First would be Lionel's wife, Judy; his daughter, Wenonah Pinn Resha; his sons, Lionel Jr., and Kenneth; Fred Fine, a former Green Beret and veteran of Korea, Vietnam, and the domestic unrest during the civil rights movement in Alabama and Mississippi. Ed Leeming, of Narragansett, Rhode Island, was generous with his time. And Army retirees Col. Clyde Sincere, Lt. Col. Ed Lesesne, and

M/Sgt. Albert Slugocki provided helpful material. My thanks also to Steve Sherman, Houston Texas.

PINN WAS A YOUNG soldier in World War II; later he became a sergeant and men who served with him would recall his leadership. Ed Leeming was in Lionel's platoon in Korea and remembered that some of the men had become irate during training. "But when we got to Korea," he said, "they thanked him, because the training saved their lives."

Similar statements were heard from veterans of Vietnam. Norman Doney recalled the rigors at Fort Bragg where Lionel Pinn became almost legendary as a physical training NCO. "He ran us all over the place," he said. "We would be running forward and Lionel would be alongside us, running backwards, smoking a cigar."

Lionel smiled at those testimonials. "You know," he said, "one of the most important moments of my career came one day when this soldier in the Special Forces came to me and said that during training he once felt like killing me. But later, in Vietnam, he said he thought about me and said the training kept him from being killed. He thanked me. That may not seem very important, but it meant a lot to me."

This is a story of war, the recollections of a remarkable soldier. But it is also the story of Lionel's personal challenge to live up to the high standards of his father, a professional soldier.

He once told me he hated war... but if there had to be one, he wanted to be there, because he was trained to deal with it. War, he said, is a reality of life on this earth. When it comes, he said, we must have well-trained soldiers.

When Lionel died in 1999 men who had been generals and colonels and sergeants and rear-rank privates came to his funeral.

Some spoke. But no words were more eloquent then those of his daughter, Wenonah, 25. His life, she said after the service, epitomized the lot of foot soldiers everywhere . . . living in mud, fierce heat or brutal winters, the combat that brings moments of high terror and flashes of sudden courage.

"Not everyone understands the 'uniqueness' of a triple Combat Infantry Badge soldier," she said. "He is the ultimate soldier, committed for life to serve his country, not by climbing the ladder to push papers and give orders, but to stay with the men who fight on the front lines. To impact young soldiers in such a way is something that words cannot explain. To dedicate one's life to being a professional soldier is rare . . . and I could not be more proud that my dad was such a man."

Frank Sikora

Hear the Bugles Calling

Prologue

Dawn crept silently across the low-slung hills, dabbling a pink glow on the heavy green tropical growth. Out in the grassy flat, beyond the row of village huts, a helicopter sat quivering, its rotating blades sending a plume of dust swirling into the air.

We hurried forward in a crouch, clutching a box full of peanut butter jars. This was Laos 1962, part of America's early involvement in Southeast Asia, a time before we entered the fire in neighboring Vietnam.

The peanut butter jars were not for making sandwiches. They were to be used in an air strike on the Communist guerrillas who were marauding through the jungles. Known as the Pathet Lao, they were trying to overthrow the government that was supported by the U.S.

Frank Taylor, my buddy and a Green Beret through and through, shouted in my ear, "We're going to be up that well-known creek if they ever start making these jars out of plastic."

I laughed, my false teeth clenched on a thick Mexican cigar. Then we clambered aboard the chopper, followed by one of our Lao soldiers who was going on the raid with us.

The peanut-butter jar attack was one way of bringing some light explosives on the Communist positions in the northern jungle of Nam Tha province, not far from the Chinese border. In March 1962 the Special Forces advisors — and there were only a few of us — didn't have an air force to speak of and we didn't have a lot of bombs to drop. But we had Yankee ingenuity.

So we concocted a way of delivering hand grenades that we could drop from the air. We pulled the pin from the grenade, held the handle down so it would not release and start the timing device, and carefully inserted it into the jar. The glass would keep the handle compressed. Then we would screw the lid on. Once we dropped them from about 800 feet, the glass would break on impact, the grenade handle would release and in a few seconds — BAM! The trick was getting them to hit near some enemy troops.

Now we were circling an area of the province that we were told harbored the Pathet Lao. They were preparing to attack a number of villages in the area. We hoped to disrupt their plans. Taylor and I stood in the doorway, leaning out as far as we dared. We went in lower, looking for signs. The idea was to draw enough fire, then zero in on the spot with the peanut butter jars as well as machine gun fire.

But after several minutes of circling, nothing happened. They weren't taking our bait. We called for the pilot to take us a little higher. As we leveled off, I picked up a jar and studied it a moment. The things can make you nervous. You can never fully trust a grenade with the pin pulled. I flipped the thing out the side, then craned my neck to watch it spin to the jungle.

Seconds later we saw a puff of smoke billowing through the branches of the trees. But nothing happened. We threw another. Still nothing. Then, from the jungle, we got a reaction.

Something hit against the side of the helicopter — Ping! Crack! — and we fell back inside.

A machine gun had opened up on us, its position marked by the string of tracer bullets that threaded a smoky chain through the morning sky, passing just above us. But a few had struck.

The Lao soldier was hit in the right shoulder by a ricochet. It spun him around and sat him down.

"I see the son-of-a-bitch," Taylor shouted. We hurled out the other jars, watching them ignite like a string of firecrackers in the green canopy of jungle growth. At the same time the side gunner opened up on the spot, spraying it with .50 caliber fire.

We tossed out the rest of the peanut butter jars and were rewarded by a line of explosions that sprouted balls of smoke. The machine gun firing came to an abrupt halt.

Not only did our improvised bombs have concussion and shrapnel in them, but the enemy troops below also had to contend with flying glass.

We suppressed the fire, and hopefully we disrupted a pending small-scale attack on a village or two — at least for a little while.

Then we headed back for camp.

MY NAME IS Lionel Francis Pinn. Laos was my third war. Most of the time I didn't fly into combat, but rather, I walked. I was always an infantry soldier.

I've won some medals, but I'm most proud of the Combat Infantryman Badge.

I earned it three times, which is a pretty rare thing. The first award was for service in World War II fighting in the Pacific. The second was for the Korean War. And the third was for service in Laos and Vietnam, where I was a Green Beret, but still a foot soldier.

The badge is blue with a silver rifle on it, and silver oak braiding around the shield. Win it twice and you get a silver star on top of it. Win it three times, and you get two silver stars. Only a few of us have done that. In the early 1990s the Army Infantry Center at Fort Benning, Ga., counted about 250 of us. By the middle 1990s, about half of them had died.

To a soldier, the Combat Infantryman Badge is the most coveted award of all . . . a Blue Badge of Courage. When I would come home from a war, civilians would point at the badge and ask, "What's that?" And I would tell them. Then they'd ask, "How many people did you kill?" And I said, "None." I don't like to talk about combat with people who were not there.

In Laos I was a sergeant, an old soldier at age thirty-eight. But it wasn't always that way.

PART ONE

WORLD WAR II

1

Born To Be a Warrior

I WAS BORN in Newton, Massachusetts, August 2, 1923, and grew up in Brookline, near Boston. My father was Master Sergeant Carl T. Pinn, a Native American. He was part Osage, part Douge. My mother, Lucy Charles Pinn, was Micmac.

There were twelve children — I was the oldest — and my father set out the rules on how we would operate. He said, "We'll help the girls along, but you boys will have to grow up and look after yourselves."

And that's how it was.

We were Catholic and though I believed in Jesus Christ as the Lord God, I also felt a strong bond to the Indian Great Spirit, which I concluded was another name for God.

When I was growing up in the 1930s my mother dearly believed that I was destined to be a priest.

I thought so, too. That is, until that July evening in 1940. We were having supper when my father told me it was time to decide my future. I was still sixteen at the time, but I would turn seventeen on August 2.

My father was stationed at nearby Fort Devens. He had fought in World War I. He was the first sergeant of a combat engineer unit.

"So what are you going to do?" he asked that night at supper.

And my mother says, "He's going to be a priest."

So he looks at me and says, "What do you say to that?"

"I think I'd like to be a priest," I said.

As a priest I could go among the Indian tribes of Maine and upstate New York and bring the word of the Church.

At the time I was 5-foot-7 inches and weighed 107 pounds. I probably couldn't do much more than try to save souls, although I had taken a few boxing lessons at the YMCA. And I was a pretty good runner, having been in the Boston Marathon a couple of times.

My father was a tall, lean but muscular man, and the fierce look he put on me made me edgy. Then he said:

"You're not the biggest guy in the world, I'll grant you that. But there's nothing wrong with your trigger finger. Boy, you need to go into the Army and grow up a bit. It'll be good for you. Three or four years there won't hurt. Besides, they'll draft you anyway. We'll probably be in another war soon."

The world was already in a lot of trouble. Hitler had conquered Poland and most of Europe. There was lots of talk that when he attacked England, America would be at war.

A few days after my father decided my career, I visited the Army Recruiting Station, passed a physical, and was sworn in.

I said goodbye to my few friends. I didn't have a girlfriend at the time. When I was younger, a kid, my girlfriend was Marie Tallchief, who was also an Indian.

She and I had grown up together and it was generally assumed by both families that one day we might marry, if I didn't become a priest. She was a beautiful girl, tall and trim, with long black hair. She looked like the classic Indian princess.

At that time I had a basic understanding of my Indian heritage, but not as much as I should have. I didn't appreciate it the way I should. When I was a boy my grandfather, Joe Charles, would tell me one of the worst dishonors for a warrior was to be taken captive, rating only behind cowardice.

"A captured warrior must always do what he can to escape," Joe Charles would say. "A dishonored warrior could never walk free in the afterlife."

Grandfather was Micmac; when he told me these things, he would look into the distant hills of Massachusetts, as though he was seeing our ancestors who had lived here centuries before the white men came. Sometimes he would take me for long walks into the forests and teach me about surviving there, to build quick fires that gave off little smoke, to fish, to find good berries to eat, to build a lean-to.

"What if you can't find anything to eat?" I once asked him.

He laughed at that. Grandfather was a handsome man. His face was brown and weathered, and had deep lines in it. His hair was gray. So when I asked him about the food, he said:

"A Micmac warrior would live on water and air, gaining a spiritual strength from the wind."

And he taught me a basic Indian lesson of escape — don't go the obvious way. Go in the opposite direction for a time and throw your pursuers off. Then, cut back around. When he would tell me those things in the early 1930s, I would hope that the day would never come when I had to face capture.

2

Entering the Army

I TOOK BASIC training at Fort Banks, Mass., and my first day in the Army taught me that I didn't know as much about the military as I had thought. A drill sergeant shouted at me to hustle it up, and when I said, "Yes, sergeant," I thought he was going to knock my head off.

I knew better than to call him "sir," because only an officer is called that. But this sergeant jumped on me because I didn't say "sergeant" loud enough.

"You speak up so you can be heard, boy," he shouted. "You're going to be a soldier and you're going to talk like a soldier or I'm gonna kick your behind half way to China. You understand me?"

I shouted loudly several times, "Yes, sergeant!"

The rifle I was issued, a World War I-era Springfield bolt action, became the heaviest thing I had ever carried in my life. It dug into my shoulders, along with the straps of the backpack. Marching became an ordeal, and I was pressed to keep up with the other guys, most of them larger than me. The average guy was about 5'10" and probably weighed 150 to 160, with some even larger. But few of them were really large.

America was still in the Depression, and many of the boys who had enlisted or been drafted looked somewhat emaciated, having lived on beans and cornbread. Most of them smoked cigarettes, and when we would get a break, they would immediately fetch a pack from their pockets or a tobacco bag and paper and roll their own. I detested the smell of cigarettes, but liked a good Cuban cigar.

Sometimes some of the smart-mouthed guys would refer to me as "pint-size" or "squirt." It was usually good-natured, but I didn't like it.

After six weeks of training, I was assigned to Fort Devens, Mass., and made a messenger with Company G, 18th Regiment, 1st Infantry Division. It meant driving around on a motorcycle, one of those with a side seat. I did fine until one day I opened up the thing to see how fast it might go and lost control rounding a curve. In a split second, I was ramming over a battalion headquarters sign and slamming into a barracks building.

That ended my career in the 1st Infantry Division. A few days later there were orders assigning me to cook's school at Camp Lee, Virginia. It looked a lot like Fort Devens with light brown barracks buildings built in a square formation around a large drill field or assembly area. The whistle to wake up came each morning before daybreak.

My second day there the sergeant-in-charge gave me the dubious honor of naming me an acting corporal, which meant wearing a blue band around the right arm. As acting corporal, I was to oversee the clean-up of the barracks and ensure that everyone got up in the morning and fell out for roll call.

A couple of nights later the sergeant told me to have the men police up the area and scrub barracks, for there was to be an inspection the next morning.

"All right, everyone, on your feet," I said quietly. "We gotta get this place spruced up."

Most of them got up and began the task. But one young, Italian-looking fellow whom the others called "Rock," lay on his bunk, his head resting on his arms.

"Come on, mister," I said, "we have to shape this place up."

He didn't move. Then he said to me, "You want it cleaned up, you clean it up."

The place went silent. My authority was being challenged.

So I asked him again to help.

He said, "You want to try to make me work? Good luck."

My father always told me that if there was going to be a fight, get on with it and don't waste time arguing. "Just hit 'em," he had said.

So I bent quickly and grabbed him by his arm and attempted to drag him off the bunk.

Like a flash he was on his feet and next thing I knew he had thrown a straight left jab that caught me on the chin and set me down on my butt. Dazed, I shook my head. But now Rock was laughing. So was everyone else in the barracks. I forced a grin, still keeping my eyes on him.

Now Rock held out his hand and helped me to my feet. "Hey, kid, you got guts. You're a little guy and you're all right: But you should learn to box. It'll help you out some later, okay? Don't ever let some jerk sucker punch you, kid."

I took Rock's advice and enrolled in a post boxing course. By then, I had been in the Army for more than four months, and had put on a little weight as well as some muscles in my arms. It took me awhile to pick up the style, but eventually I began throwing hard straight left jabs, and fast right crosses.

Soon I began to feel a confidence in myself that had never

before existed. I might not be a match for someone like Rock, but I could handle myself with the average guy.

During that time I learned to be an Army cook, getting up at four o'clock each morning to scramble about four hundred eggs and make a barrel of coffee. It wasn't bad work and I usually had time off in the afternoon to go to the gym and train.

I might have been a better boxer if it had not been for a girl named Virginia Moffit, who was about seventeen. I met her at a skating rink off post and soon lost my interest in boxing. She was the first woman in my life. On New Year's Eve we were secretly married.

Her father was a well-to-do business executive who hated me from day one. He made no bones about it, either.

"I don't want you hanging around with some buck-ass private," he told Virginia as she prepared to go out with me one night. "I want you to marry a Navy officer."

When he found out about the marriage, he went berserk. Virginia lived in an apartment near the fort, and when I was off duty I would spend time with her. But it was clear that her family's discontent over the marriage was wearing on her.

One day I came to the apartment and found a note that she had left. It said she wanted a divorce. In fact, it was later simply annulled.

It was just as well. That same day I had been summoned to the orderly room and told by the top sergeant, a big ruddy-faced man, that I was on orders to be transferred to Camp Sheridan, Ill.

I packed my things again and rode a train to Illinois. There, orders put me in an R&P (receiving and processing) center, to be assigned where and when I was needed. Why they sent me there I would never know.

But I did know that it would change my life for the worst, at least for the time being. I was put in a barracks with a guy who let the temporary corporal band on his arm go to his head. He was a tall, dark-haired fellow we called "Hollywood," because of his fine looks and haughty bearing.

When we were marching he shouted at us, calling us sad examples of soldiers. One day he aimed his insults at me:

"Get in step, Shorty," he snapped. I bristled, but stared straight ahead.

That evening at supper I sat at the same long table as Hollywood. Meals were served family style, with the plates of food placed at each table. I was hungry and quickly ate up a helping of ham and cabbage, beans, and mashed potatoes. It was good and I wanted more.

Speaking to no one in particular, I said, "Pass the potatoes."

Hollywood picks up the bowl and he says, "You want potatoes? Then you get potatoes."

And with that he threw the bowl hard. It struck me in the chest, and potatoes spilled over my shirt and onto my lap. My first reaction was surprise and disbelief. Some of the other guys were laughing at me.

"When you want potatoes," Hollywood was saying, "you say, 'Please pass the potatoes.' You don't order people around. That'll teach you to remember to say 'please.'"

I was on my feet in a flash, not really thinking about my actions. I saw the surprised look on Hollywood's face, and then I was upon him, a left jab shooting out and striking him square on the jaw.

By then some of the men grabbed me and pulled me back, while others tended to Hollywood. The Military Police were called and I was taken away to the post stockade, a grim set of barracks surrounded by barbed wire fencing. A couple of days later a hearing was held by the Provost Marshal's staff and a captain ordered me confined for thirty days. It was an unusually stern sentence for hitting another private who had hit me first. I felt that I was the victim of an unjust punishment because of my Indian blood.

The more I sat in the stockade and stewed about it, the angrier I became. After twenty-five days the MPs came to my room and unlocked the door and told me I was free to return to the processing center.

I got my things without a word and walked briskly to the barracks, found Hollywood, and hit him again, the blow knocking him out of the barracks window. They hurried Hollywood to the post hospital, and they hauled me back to the stockade.

ON THE THIRD DAY I was told Hollywood was in serious but stable condition. An MP told me to shave, clean up and prepare for a court martial. I didn't have a prayer. The witnesses told what they had seen that day.

On the stand I testified that I wasn't trying to throw Hollywood out the window, he simply fell out when he was hit. It wasn't a convincing statement; I was found guilty and sentenced to a year of hard labor. They shipped me to Camp Ellis, Illinois. There, I was placed in a wire compound with a bunch of wacky acting men who were probably the scum of the Army. They were men who had tried to kill or maim others, or had been guilty of attempted rape. They were not the kind of people I wanted as friends.

The next morning we were summoned to formation, then told to begin our work detail. Two MPs were assigned to my group; one held a shotgun while the other attached a chain to my ankle. The chain stretched about 36 inches. At the end was a sixteen-pound iron ball.

"This'll be part of your uniform from now on, Lionel," the guard said.

Then I limped to a truck and struggled aboard. We were driven to a barren stretch of land that was full of whitish rock. I was given a sledge hammer and told to begin breaking them up.

"What's this stuff for?" I asked.

"It's for Colgate tooth powder," one of the MPs said. "We supply them from here. You didn't know that?"

"I didn't know where it came from," I said.

It wasn't until a few days had gone by that I realized that I had been the object of a joke: The busted rock was not used to make Colgate tooth powder. But the imprisonment, the pointless hard labor, and the ball and chain left me cold and bitter. I believed that I had drawn the severe sentence in the first place because I was Indian. The white soldiers had made an example of me.

I hated the Army; I hated white people; I had contempt for the Indian spirit of honor that I had been taught. Where was the honor now? Who cared for me now that I was a prisoner? And why was I a prisoner in the first place? It wasn't fair.

All over a plate of potatoes...

During my months in stockade, I received only two letters from my mother. She said she would pray for me. My father would say nothing to me, and Mother said he was disappointed. He was ashamed. I could only imagine that Grandfather Joe was sickened by the fact I was a stockade bum. After all the things he had told me about being a captive . . . .

Finally, in early November 1941, I was told to pack my things, that my time was up. An MP removed the ball and chain from my right leg. I felt like a newborn baby. I was light and free. As

I was processed out, an MP sergeant muttered to me, "Stay out of trouble, Pinn. It's a lot easier being a good soldier than a bad one. I hope we don't see you back here."

I glanced at him and nodded. "I've had enough of this place. In fact, I've had enough of the Army. When my time's up, I'm gettin' out."

The MP laughed and said, "We all may be here a lot longer than we think. The Army's not a bad life. Three slops and a flop. Enjoy yourself."

That MP must have paid closer attention to world affairs than me.

3

Pearl

THE ARMY RETURNED me to Fort Devens, Mass., which meant I could spend some time with my family. When I arrived home my mother greeted me warmly, but my father had little to say to me. He would come home on the weekends.

"Messed up, didn't you," was the extent of it. Later, he added, "You still have time to make something of yourself, although I don't think you've got what it takes. You have a long way to go, boy."

I respected my father, but I felt he was not being fair to me. A kind word would have helped me over the bad bumps I had just taken. But my father, the master sergeant, never let up.

It would be the beginning of a long and arduous trail in which I would try to live up to his expectations, not that I ever thought I would be able to manage it.

On weekends I would go out and try to find some fun. One Friday night I went to a skating rink in the south part of Boston and met an attractive girl named Pearl. She went to college and worked part time. After spending months in a stockade, it was nice to share time with a nice girl who had a gift for being a good talker and listener.

We skated a few hours, then went to a small restaurant for coffee and doughnuts.

Pearl was a tall, slim girl with long brunette hair and big brown eyes.

She glanced up from her coffee and saw me studying her features.

"I'm Jewish," she said, "in case you're wondering."

"That's nothing," I told her. "I'm Indian."

She grinned. "What does that have to do with anything?"

I told her about my brief marriage. She nodded solemnly. Then she changed the subject.

"What does everyone call you?" she asked. "Do you have a nickname or is it just 'Lionel'? Or what's your middle name?"

"Francis," I said. "It's after St. Francis of Assisi. He liked animals and birds. But my mom calls me Lionel."

"What do you do in the Army?" she asked. "You haven't told me much about it."

I laughed. "I help make Colgate tooth powder."

"Colgate tooth powder? Are you serious?"

"Naw, not really," I said. "That's a private joke."

"By a private," she said, noting that my uniform had no stripes on the sleeves.

The following weekend we dated again, meeting at the rink, whirling around the floor to the recorded music of Glenn Miller and Benny Goodman.

The next day, Sunday Dec. 7, I went to the restaurant near the skating rink and I heard some of the guys talking about "Pearl getting bombed."

I thought at first they were talking about my girl, that she had gotten drunk, i.e., "bombed."

Then came the clarification: The U.S. Navy base at Pearl Harbor had been bombed by the Japanese. We were at war.

The world changed then. The Army I had known ceased to exist; all the brass polishing and shoe shining and scrubbing floors took a back seat. Everything began to move at a rapid pace. On Christmas Eve I went to see Pearl and asked her to marry me. I wanted her for my wife, before the Army sent me overseas.

When I asked her, she told me she would have to have the permission of her parents. We went to their home and Pearl eased into the kitchen, leaving me in the living room with her father.

"So you want to ask me something?" he said.

I nodded. "I've asked Pearl to marry me. But she said she needs your permission."

He didn't answer, but stood up, then gestured. "Come with me."

I followed him down a hallway. Then he opened the bathroom door and gestured for me to follow. When I entered, he turned.

"Unzip your pants," he said. "Get it out."

"What?"

I stared at him. What was this guy, a queer or something? If he wasn't Pearl's father I would have decked him.

"Just do it," he said. "I just want to see something."

Hesitating, I finally unzipped my pants and flopped it out.

He glanced down, then quickly turned away. "All right. Zip up. You can't marry my daughter."

"Why not?"

"You haven't been circumcised. You're not Jewish."

"Well, I beg your pardon, sir, but what's important is that I love her."

He waved his hand cutting off the discussion and returned to his chair in the living room, picked up a newspaper and proceeded to ignore me. Afterwards, Pearl came out and we left, walking along the streets and looking at holiday lights. She walked close to me against the cold of the night. Snow flurries drifted by the street lights.

"He says you can't marry me," I said.

"I know," she replied. "So what now?"

"I think we can make up our own minds," I said. "I think if you want to marry me, you should. We'll just go away."

"I can't do that," she said. "I can't go against my family. Let's just enjoy ourselves one day at a time."

We returned to her home and sat up talking until the wee hours. Then I left.

Over the following weeks I waited for an order sending me overseas. Here at last would be a chance to prove myself to my father. I would fight with the best of them. Within a few days I received new orders: I was to help in the processing and training of new recruits. My part would be to cook and oversee the trainees pulling KP. It hardly seemed like much of a part in the war effort. I wanted to go overseas and fight.

Through early 1942 I remained at Fort Devens, but I kept requesting transfers to the infantry. Finally, late in the winter, the Army ordered me to Fort Ord, Calif., a post overlooking the Pacific. I was to help train raw recruits to be infantry soldiers.

The orders came hurriedly and I rushed to the coffee shop to meet Pearl and say goodbye. We had less than twenty minutes.

"I'm shipping out," I said. "I don't know if it means going to the Pacific or what. There's a lot of worry about California being invaded."

She shook her head, blinked several times, and shrugged. "I

guess in wartime you just can't make plans for anything. They never work out. You just take care of yourself. Don't do anything foolish."

"I'll write to you," I said.

She nodded.

"I'll meet you back here one day, OK?" I hugged her. "We'll pick up where we left off."

She forced a smile. "I'll count on that."

When you're a soldier there's just not time to do the things you feel you want to do. Everything was in a frantic pace.

Pearl kissed me on the cheek and walked away. I think she didn't want me to see that she was crying. I would never see her again.

4

Combat: New Guinea

I was on a train for four days, finally arriving at Fort Ord on a misty, cool morning in April 1942. My boxing training, limited as it was, nevertheless made me a candidate to help prepare others. The boxing moves helped me teach recruits to use the bayonet, to pivot and dance from one foot to the other, and lunge with the body, thrusting the weapon forward.

I became a good bayonet instructor, often called upon by drill sergeants to demonstrate the technique to the trainees.

"The spirit of the bayonet is to kill," I shouted at them. "You shoot first, but if you get in a tight, the bayonet will be your best friend. Know how to use it."

During that period of training I grew up, not only in size, but in my mind, I think. By the winter of 1942 I was 5'8" and weighed 150 pounds. My stomach was hard and flat, and I carried little or no fat. I wanted to be a professional soldier after all, like my father, although at the time I didn't have a lot of choice; in World War II you were in "for the duration." I had no idea how long we might be at war. There was concern that the Japanese might bomb or even land troops along the West Coast. Some of the men predicted that the war might last ten to fifteen years.

One afternoon after a bayonet training session, I went to the orderly room and asked to be sent to where the fighting was.

The commanding officer refused, telling me I was needed to train men to fight with the bayonet.

But one day in the summer of 1943 I was told to report to company headquarters. The sergeant told me to have a seat. Then the captain called, "Send in that hotshot bayonet instructor ."

I walked in, came to attention, snapped a salute, and called, "Private Pinn reporting, sir."

"At ease," he said, tossing a salute. "All right, Pinn, you want to go fight the enemy. I guess there's a place for you. You'll be on orders within ten days. I hope your Japanese is good. Dismissed."

In July 1943 I was finally put on orders to go to the Pacific as an infantry replacement. I formally reenlisted in the Army for three more years, then boarded a ship. It took forty-four days to reach our destination — New Guinea.

My first view of it revealed a God-forsaken place, hot and rainy, steamy fog hanging over the thick jungles, and swarms of bugs. We unloaded at Port Moresby and I was sent north to a region called Buna, a former jungle site that had been touched by civilization. American Seebees had bulldozed it flat and pushed away the palm trees and the tons of warty vines and heavy undergrowth.

There were quonset huts and tents in all directions; sun-tanned men clad only in shorts and floppy green caps slogged through the mud paths, swatting at mosquitoes and cursing the heat. I was assigned to the Sixth Army Headquarters and after several weeks of indoctrination and training was put in the replacement pool for one of the infantry divisions operating on the island.

A sergeant took some of us in tow one day and gave us some advice:

"It's a hell of a lot different place than America," he said. "You remember two things out here. One, don't get yourself killed. And the second, if a monkey eats something, it's OK for you to eat. If he won't eat it, you can't eat it. One thing more. Watch out for crocodiles. They're bigger than tanks. They'll eat you alive. Stay out of the rivers."

NEW GUINEA IS one of the largest islands in the world, about 1,200 miles across. Looking at it on a map, it resembles the shape of a bird, with the head at the northwest corner. The center part is mountainous, with the Owen Stanley Range cutting across; the coastal zones are hot and humid, with thick jungle growth, alternating with plains of high grass. The island inhabitants were primitive people who mostly wore little or no clothing and worshipped the sun. Some groups were known to be head-hunters. A few had been taught Christianity by the Dutch colonists.

We were here because the Japanese invaded the island in 1942 and built airfields. They planned to use New Guinea as a staging ground for an invasion of Australia, which lies to the south. Buna, on the northeast part of New Guinea, was now in American hands; hard fighting had been going on for months. It would go on for many more. In all, there were about 200,000 American troops taking part in the action on New Guinea, maybe more. Unlike some of the other Pacific battles, the one for New Guinea would not take days or even weeks, but more than two years.

One night we gathered in the command tent and were given a briefing on a scouting patrol the next day. About fifteen of us were going. We were going to check an area in the northern section. The mission was to locate an American fighter pilot who had been shot down. We hoped we could find him alive.

The other men were mostly known by nicknames. They called me "Chief," the name given to most American Indians. I smoked cigars when I could find them (actually I had smoked my first one when I was six years old), and the smoke puffing up above me reminded them of smoke signals, so they said.

You could say my first taste of combat was simply trying to cut my way through the thick, swampy underbrush that covered much of the place. Dark muck sucked at my feet, bugs bit me, I tripped over huge roots that lay above ground. But for days I never saw a Japanese soldier, much less shot at one.

The first enemy soldier I saw was a dead one who lay along a path near the base of the mountains. His entrails, a sickly bluish-yellow, had spilled out and were rotting; his swollen body seemed about to burst through the tattered uniform. Holding my breath against the stench, I stepped by without a glance. That night we camped without a fire, eating cold rations and taking turns keeping watch.

WE RESUMED OUR patrol the next morning. I was in the middle of the column. The scout, or point man, was the guy out front. His job was to locate enemy positions, like machine gun nests. Often the lead scout might get within ten feet of a machine gun.

The way you found it was when the Japanese gunner opened up—usually on the scout.

I was armed with a Thompson submachine gun, commonly known as a Tommy gun. I preferred it to the Garand M-1 rifle, which was a semi-automatic weapon. The M-1 was accurate, but it fired only eight rounds before you had to reload. The Tommy gun was automatic, firing ten rounds in a second; it held fifty bullets, but could hold a larger drum that held 90.

On this morning, fog settled over the heavy canopy of

growth and swirled into it, settling down almost on the ground; the sounds of the jungle became more intense. We each carried a package of K rations, which was made up of some crackers and a small container of cheese. We also had a canteen full of water. That was essential. I didn't have to be reminded of that. I learned to carry two canteens of water and extra ammuntion. As long as I had water, I could survive. Like Grandfather Joe Charles had said, a warrior can live on air and water.

After two hours, with the sun climbing higher and the air hot and steamy, we moved off the rugged trail and the man in front of me signaled for me to get down. I turned and passed the signal back. The jungle was alive with sound: birds chattering, monkeys babbling, insects buzzing.

I unfastened a canteen from its holder and took a deep long drink. About two minutes had passed when something in the jungle changed. Just what, I didn't know. But the chattering became more subdued and some birds quickly took flight. I sensed something was wrong and hurriedly replaced my canteen in its holder.

Grandfather Joe Charles had always told me that when the wild things in the forests change their pattern, something is happening or about to happen. There was an awful stillness and I slowly moved my finger to the safety release on my Tommy gun. It made a slight click sound, but in the frozen heat of the moment, it sounded like a firecracker.

The other men that I could see were also in a tense body set, all peering into the green canopy ahead. It occurred to me that I was not afraid. Excited, tense, yes. But not afraid.

Suddenly, from somewhere in front, came a bone-chilling shriek, a sound that made my back quiver like electricity had run along the spine. The shout was followed almost instantly by a grenade exploding and a burst of rifle and machine gun fire. I rolled to the side and went flat, just as shrapnel and bullets sent green foliage drifting over me. I didn't feel fear, just a cold tightness that clutched my stomach and made my mouth dry. My eyes searched the dense growth, but I could find no Japanese to shoot at. Nothing but green.

Then another flurry of rifle shots clattered through the moist air, and again bullets whizzed nearby; another grenade exploded, a dull, muffled WHOOMPF! sound that sent a concussion wave through the undergrowth. I heard one of our men up ahead groan, "I'm hit, I'm hit."

Things got chaotic in a hurry. The sergeant was shouting, "Someone get up there and pull him back. Stay low."

There was another eruption of rifle fire from the invisible Japanese soldiers. They seemed to be about twenty-five yards away, maybe less.

I didn't wait any longer. I rolled a few times through thick vines and figured to come up and shoot. But I managed to get my weapon tangled. "Damn it," I muttered. Pulling it free, I aimed ahead to the right, where the shots came from, and fired a two-second burst.

Some of the other men began firing. I fought my way out of the tangle of vines, remembering it wasn't a good idea to stay in one place if there was no cover. The vines concealed me, but they offered no protection if I was fired upon. There is a difference.

But then it was over as quicky as it had begun. The shooting stopped. The sergeant cautiously signaled us to back down the trail, hauling the one wounded man with us. He had been hit in the lower abdomen. It was a broad wound, inflicted, I was told, by a grenade explosion. The blast had ripped into his guts. His face was a ghostly white; he lay still on a poncho as we strained to carry him. I was sure he would die. The smell of raw flesh, mixed with the odor of gunpowder, seemed to mingle with the sweat coating my skin.

The return trip was slower, because of the wounded man; the heat had become oppressive. Earlier we had passed a small clearing. When we reached it again, we paused to rest.

My mouth was dry and I undid the canteen again, drinking the warm water. I had just capped it when a loud popping sound erupted just a few yards away. I dove away from the other men, rolled once and lay prone.

Then I saw something that made me almost jump out of my skin. Just fifteen or twenty yards away, was a Japanese soldier, standing in the midst of some overhanging vines. It seemed as though he appeared from nowhere. He was just there. He saw me at the same time and quickly raised his rifle and pointed it my way.

"Japs!" I shouted. At the same time I raised the Tommy gun with my right hand and fired blindly, without aiming. It was simply a reflex reaction. But the burst hit the guy right in the chest. Blood sprayed out and he was jerked violently backwards as though by an invisible cord. He sprawled on his back.

There were shouts from the jungle, several more shots, then silence. I waited, my weapon ready, looking to see some sign of movement expecting at any moment that a wave of Japanese soldiers might burst upon us. This could be the day I was going to die. But after about five minutes someone called softly, "Looks clear."

We nervously raised from the ground and moved forward. The dead Japanese soldier stared vacantly at the sky. I gazed down at him, now feeling somewhat stunned by the suddenness of it. In a split second he was dead. It could just as easily have been me.

The lieutenant who led the patrol ordered a party of four to carry the wounded man back to our lines, while the rest of us maintained a watch. After fifteen minutes, it appeared the enemy had fled. Then I walked up to the dead Japanese soldier for a closer look. I felt inside his shirt and found a small piece of orange cloth that contained lettering on it, probably his name and the names of his family. I pulled it free and folded it up, putting it in my shirt pocket.

Before leaving I took one final look at him. He appeared to be in his early 20s, maybe 25. I had wanted to fight them with a passion at one time. Now there was just an empty feeling.

We went back without locating the American pilot.

THE THING ABOUT New Guinea was that we didn't know exactly where we were. We would just go into the jungle and be gone for days. It rained often and it rained hard. Sleep was almost impossible. At least a halfway comfortable sleep. It was sometimes hard to tell when you were at the "front," because it didn't always exist in the sense that there were established lines, with a clearly marked "no-man's land" in between.

We would go for days and not see the enemy. Sometimes we would go to a "rear area" for rest, and find ourselves under attack. Those of us who were rear-tank privates in the infantry were not alone in the perplexity of the situation. Maj. Gen. Walter Krueger, the commander of Sixth Army, would later write that he was vexed by the enormity of the island and the diversity of the terrain, that units were scattered and flung from jungle swamps to mountain tops to islands. Apparently, the Army was having a hard time keeping the paperwork up with the changing situation.

ONE DAY I was assigned to help guard our planes at one of the fields the engineers and Seebees had carved out of the jungle. I think the Japanese had built one first, but we took it. I was there with my Tommy gun when this pilot came out and introduced himself. He was Maj. Richard Bong, one of the aces.

"Sir, how many Jap planes have you shot down?" I asked.

"Not many," he said. "What I want is a Japanese souvenir to take home. You guys on the ground get all the souvenirs."

"We get all the breaks," I said.

He laughed. "Well, if you get an extra one, I'll pay you for it. See if you can get me one of those swords."

There have always been stories about how the infantry didn't care for the Air Corps or later the Air Force. But I never found that to be true. The infantry I was with always respected the airmen because they put their lives on the line to help us.

Several days later I was sent on a patrol into the Owen Stanley Range to search for a large American plane that went down, with 17 personnel aboard. The mission was to rescue them if they were alive — or if they weren't, to bring the bodies back. There was also some technical equipment on the plane which we were to retrieve or destroy so the Japanese wouldn't find it.

It took five days to get to the plane; all the men were dead, their bodies badly decomposed in the jungle heat. We didn't actually see the plane until we were almost on top of it, the jungle was so thick.

It seemed it swallowed up the machine. We covered the bodies with rubber ponchos and put blankets over them, placed them on stretchers and started back.

One night it rained hard and the air was chilly. I was miserable and wanted to find a dry place to sleep. I took one of the blankets from one of the dead guys.

"What the hell you doing?" a sergeant asked.

"Trying to keep warm," I said. "He doesn't need it anymore. He can't feel the rain."

On the third night just as we prepared to stop and make camp, a Japanese patrol came across us and opened fire. A mortar shell exploded and I felt a stinging, burning sensation in my left leg, above the knee. I fell next to one of the bodies and almost vomited from the stench.

Hurt, bleeding, dying, I didn't care, I got up and hobbled away and dove for cover behind a tree. I had to get away from the odor. Enemy fire ripped through the brush. Men were yelling to take cover, they were yelling to return fire, yelling where the fire was coming from, and just yelling.

In a couple of minutes, it was over. I was aware that my leg was bleeding heavily and seemed to be swelling. A medic put some bandages on it and gave me a pain pill. The night settled back down to the usual jungle sounds and heat. I dozed off. It was daylight when I awoke; the men were putting me on a stretcher, arguing about who was going to carry it. I was still kind of floating from the pain medicine. It was rugged country, with steep ridges along the trail, occasional Japanese snipers, and almost daily rainfalls.

As they carried me along, the worsening smell of the dead men filled the air and made me sick.

"Damn it, put me up front," I said, "so I won't have to smell that."

It took them another three days to get me to a field hospital. The wounds had healed somewhat, but I had come down with a fever caused by some tropical bug, and was delirious for several days. During that time I lost about fifteen pounds. When I returned to duty my cheek bones protruded sharply and my clothes felt like they belonged to a giant.

But in two weeks I was back to near normal and ordered to active duty again. One night some of the guys wanted to celebrate and said they were going to fix me a "real man's" drink.

"Go get some gasoline," a sergeant said.

One of them returned shortly with a small can of gas. Meanwhile the sergeant had obtained several loaves of thick Army bread. They added something to the gasoline and then poured it all through the bread, straining it. After it had dripped through, the sergeant poured some in a canteen and handed it to me.

"Here," he said, "have you a real drink."

The others sat and watched, big grins on their faces.

"Like hell," I said. "You can't drink gasoline."

"You can if it's been strained through Army bread," the sergeant said. The others laughed.

With some hesitation I took the cup, then took a sip. Then I swallowed it. It was like molten lava going down my throat.

"Holy hell," I said. "That's real firewater."

They laughed. Then, I took another drink. "That's enough," said the sergeant. "Don't want to get too much."

Then he drank some. It was the damnest thing I ever heard of. I never knew whether it was really gasoline they used or if they slipped something else in there, and played a joke on me. But whatever it was, I survived. I would not advise anyone else to try it.

LIKE MOST AMERICANS, I guess, I had a hatred for the Japanese military regime that had caused such misery for the world. But at the frontline level, it wasn't so much a personal hatred as a will to fight and a determination to win. But as we were taught, all Japs were bad and they were the enemy. They had no respect for life — ours or theirs.

But the oddest thing happened to me that changed my viewpoint a little. We were taking a break while on patrol when suddenly we heard shouts coming, it seemed, from all directions, and rifle and machine gunfire erupted. We had been bushwhacked by a Japanese patrol in force that quickly got some of our men and sent the others rushing away. A grenade fragment had caught me in the arm.

Meantime a second grenade landed nearby and the impact knocked me down. I knew I was hurt, but not badly. Yet I couldn't seem to move. Everything was in a daze. Next thing I knew a couple of Japanese soldiers pulled me to my feet and gave me a shove.

They forced me to dogtrot through the thick jungle. I grew weak and fell a couple of times and thought I might die right there. The Japanese soldiers would shout and prod me up, using their rifle butts. Finally they got me to some kind of encampment, a clearing in the jungle, where they had some little tents and a few crude wooden structures thrown up. Nearby was a river, which I gathered to be the Sepik, based on my recollection of a map of the area. There were several Americans sitting behind a little fenced enclosure.

The place smelled like something was rotting. I was thirsty; it was hard to swallow and my tongue felt like it was swollen. I asked for water and a guard shoved me toward the gate of the fenced area. My wounds were infected and I grew weaker. I vaguely was aware that two soldiers dragged me across the small compound and threw water on my face, then when I roused, handed me a container of warm water. I drank it.

Later I was taken by guards and tied to a banana tree. Then, a Japanese lieutenant began questioning me. I gave my name, rank, and serial number. A guard began pulling out my fingernails.

To be truthful, it hurt badly and I'm not too proud to admit I began to cry like a baby. I kept telling them my name, rank, and serial number.

Just then I heard a voice from nearby, a voice speaking in almost perfect English.

"I recognize that accent," the voice said. "You're from New England."

Now the guards backed away and I looked through the blur of tears and saw a Japanese captain, who appeared to be in his forties. The man walked closer. "You know how I knew that accent?" he asked. "Because I went to Harvard."

I was puzzled, but God knows very much relieved. I stared at the man.

"You know where Harvard is?" he asked.

I nodded. "Yeah, I know."

He said he was the camp commander and his name was Yamashita. I stared at him with some skepticism, wary of an enemy officer who appeared too friendly. But then the guy issued some orders in Japanese and the guards cut me loose, and soon a medic showed up and began tending to my hands and also the wounds that had crusted and become infected. The guards then took me back to the little compound and gave me the usual ration of rice and pieces of raw fish.

A couple of days went by and then the guards were back, telling me to get up and follow them. They took me to the camp headquarters, a rickety wood building with a small oil lamp on the desk. The captain was there and told me to sit down.

"Have you killed any Japanese soldiers?" he asked.

I shook my head and lied. "No. None that I know of."

"When the war is over," he said, "I hope to go back to Harvard and continue my studies. I enjoyed being in Boston and visiting the towns in the area. Is your family still there?"

I nodded, then concluding that it would be of no military value, I said, "We live in Brookline."

"I've been there," he said. "The Charles River. When I was in Boston I met a beautful young woman and we were friends." He paused for a moment, staring beyond me. "Everyone wants to be an American," he continued. "In Japan, my family is bound by tradition. They do not accept some of my thinking. In America you can be free to do as you please, to go to a bar, or a club. And you don't have to take off your shoes. And you can be with someone who is different."

"I'm Indian," I said. "I dated a Jewish girl."

He nodded. Then he stood up. "Follow me," he said.

We went outside and he headed for a path that led to the river. I was aware of two guards walking behind me, their rifles at port arms. I didn't know where we were going, or for what purpose. Then we reached the water's edge. I hesitated. I knew they were going to shoot me and I thought about making a break.

The Japanese officer gestured to the river. "Are you a good swimmer?"

I stared at him. Then I nodded, slowly. "Pretty good."

As I watched he took a rifle from one of the guards. This was it, I thought. He was going to shoot me. He raised the weapon and fired one shot — into the water. Then he fired another. I stood there, glancing from the water back to the officer.

Then, handing the weapon back to the soldier, he gestured downriver. "Go now."

I was dumbfounded. He was letting me go. Still thinking I might be shot for an attempted escape, I backed into the water, watching the guards. They turned their backs. I took one last look at the officer.

He stared at me then said, "See you in Boston."

Then he turned and walked away.

I dove into the water and began swimming with the current. God, I was free. I couldn't believe it. I vaguely recalled the stories about big crocodiles, but I went under, and swam as far as I could, came up quickly for air, then went under again. I couldn't be sure there weren't Japanese troops on the banks, waiting to take a pot shot at me.

But then I reasoned that it would make no sense, that if the Japanese wanted to shoot me, they could have done it easily enough. There had been countless stories of atrocities committed against Americans. A downed pilot, we were told, had been beheaded by a Japanese officer. Why I was allowed to walk away, I would never know for sure. The only explanation was that I was Indian and from New England.

For two days I swam the river and crawled along the banks. Finally, I saw a group of Seebees working on a project of some kind. I had heard some "hells" and "damns." They were a most welcome sound and a most welcome sight.

The Japanese had committed numerous atrocities in the Pacific. It was clear to me that the Japanese captain was a rare exception; in later years fellow veterans would find it difficult to comprehend. But war brings strange events.

THE FIGHTING IN New Guinea seemed like it would go on forever. During these times American units were loading onto boats and making landings along the northern coast of New Guinea at places like Hollandia, as well as the offshore islands.

It was during this time that I was asked if I wanted to volunteer for training with an elite Sixth Army group known as the "Alamo Scouts." This was a special unit that operated in small teams, usually behind enemy lines, scouting and collecting information. The group had been the brainchild of Gen. Krueger, who wanted a commando-like unit to obtain intelligence information first hand.

It sounded interesting and I volunteered. The training course was six weeks at a place called Fergusson Island off the northeast coast of New Guinea. It was almost an island paradise. Col. Frederick Bradshaw, a lawyer from Jackson, Miss., was commander. We spent a lot of time swimming and running. There was also intensive scouting and patrolling training, night exercises, and even some language courses, to help us talk with the natives.

The Alamo Scouts would become the forerunners of what would later be known as Special Forces, or the Green Berets. Some of those who trained remained with the Alamo Scouts, others went back to home units to be Scouts.

The Army assigned me to a demolition unit, training me to blow things up: bridges, houses, bunkers, anything that could be blown. One day I was on a patrol in force when we ran into a trouble spot. It was a Japanese machine gun nest situated halfway up a grassy hill, dotted with trees that had been splintered by artillery fire.

The bullets that go over your head don't whistle; instead they create a loud snapping or popping sound. The whistling comes when one hits a rock and ricochets. I pushed my helmet back so I could see. My helmet was always coming off or slipping forward. The thing was always in the way. Anyway, I moved it back, wiped dirt away from my eyes, raised my Tommy gun and began firing at the stronghold.

It was hard to tell if I was hitting close, because I would only raise up for a second or so to fire, then go flat again. To my right some of our guys had taken cover behind rocks and stubby trees that lined a shallow defile. They were prone, but even so some of the Japanese machine gun bullets were bouncing around and striking some of them.

The only thing between me and the machine gun was a slight rise in the ground and every once in a while the gunner would send a stream of bullets over my head. A little lower and they would have clipped the grass. I put another magazine in the Tommy gun, then rolled left. There wasn't time to map out what to do, but I felt something needed to be done. I wasn't really thinking. When you're in the soup, you don't think, you just act by instinct.

I crawled through the rough grass until I was about twenty-five yards away from the side of the machine gun nest, then eased up to get a better look. There were excited shouts from the interior. I eased forward to within ten yards. I had two grenades. I got one, pulled the pin, then threw it, going flat on the ground until I heard it go off. Then I jumped up with the Tommy gun aimed at the bunker and began firing. A Japanese soldier staggered out, holding his eyes. Then he slumped to the ground. Another one came from somewhere behind the bunker. I dropped him with a one-second burst.

Now I pulled the other grenade out and tossed it. I watched it hit right in front of the bunker, then fell face down, holding my helmet. The blast sent shards of shrapnel over my head. The machine gun had stopped firing. All of a sudden three Japanese soldiers tumbled out of the bunker. They saw me, shouted, and turned, raising their rifles.

I aimed the Thompson from my hip and frantically squeezed the trigger — and nothing happened. I was out of ammo. I called out in surprise, just a shout of some kind.

But it startled the Japanese and they paused for a moment.

Maybe they thought I was calling out a surrender. I don't know. But then they resumed their advance toward me.

"God Almighty," I said and threw the Tommy gun at them. It missed, but made them duck. Then I bent over and picked up a rifle lying by one of the dead Japanese soldiers. It had a fixed bayonet. By now I was sure some of the other guys would be coming up the slope to help out. I don't really know what I was thinking. But I let out a war whoop just like my ancestors — it was nothing but a loud yell, maybe something like a Rebel yell — and took a step toward the three Japanese.

They could have shot me easily enough, but I was hollering and wagging the fixed bayonet, and they stood at the ready. Then one of them lunged toward me. I faked a butt stroke to the face, then spun and pushed forward with a long thrust. The bayonet caught him in the gut; he fell backward.

The second one rushed forward. I didn't fake him, just made a short thrust at his throat, followed by another one to the midsection. But this guy was fast. He side-stepped both of my thrusts. Next thing I knew he had ducked then came up and blocked my third thrust, jabbed his bayonet at my neck, just missed, then did a sudden downward slash that caught me on the left forearm. I saw blood spurting but did not feel pain. All my energy and thoughts were on the fight, which was one to the finish. I shouted again as I side-stepped him, but he caught me on the right forearm. Two wounds! My breath came in quick gasps. I swung the rifle butt up hard; it caught him on the side of the face, with a thwacking sound. He grunted and went down to one knee, his eyes wide with just a flash of fear in them. He tried to pivot quickly, but he wasn't quick enough. I got him in the chest. He had a puzzled, anguished look in his eyes as he toppled over.

The third one was kind of a chunky guy with glasses. I shouted again, "Hey!" This guy turned and ran. I couldn't believe it. I walked away from it, throwing the Japanese rifle down. I picked up the Thompson and reloaded.

By now the other guys had cleared the slope and one of them tossed a grenade into the machine gun emplacement. I was aware some of them were talking to me but I didn't listen. I sat down under a tree. I wanted a cigar to smoke. Someone got one for me and I sat there for twenty minutes or so, puffing and thinking about home.

A medic came up and bandaged my arms. As he worked on me, I said to him, "You know, I can't believe one of 'em got me pretty good. I'm supposed to be such a tough guy with the bayonet. You know, I'm a bayonet instructor. Hell, this guy taught me some things."

Sometime later I was put in for a medal of some kind but the paperwork got lost in the shuffle. I never heard anything further about it.

5

Fighting in the Islands

BY OCTOBER 1944 the war was moving on from New Guinea, although the island itself was far from secure; it was estimated that as many as 25,000 Japanese might still be locked in among the mountains and the jungles. But they no longer had a navy to take them to Australia. In October 1944 General MacArthur sent troops to invade the Phillipines, keeping his pledge that "I shall return."

Over the many months in New Guinea I saw the General a couple of times from a distance. He was riding in a jeep. I had always viewed him as a tall, imposing figure. But actually, to my surprise, MacArthur appeared to be quite short.

On Jan. 9,1945, I went ashore assigned to the 569th Quartermaster Company, which landed along with forward combat units. The Army, suspecting that my wounds should keep me out of the front lines, had attached me to the QM outfit. It was okay and the training I had received could help me if I chose to remain in the military.

These islands weren't as wild as New Guinea, and the people were civilized, most of them speaking English. But we didn't have much chance to visit with the home folks. The Japanese were fighting as desperately as ever. A few weeks after landing the word came around asking for some volunteers to go with the 6th

Ranger Battalion and some Alamo Scouts to liberate Americans who had been held prisoners of war since the islands had been captured by the Japanese in early 1942.

I volunteered, as there would likely be a need for demolition work. I remembered my own imprisonment with the iron ball around my ankle, and I knew that was nothing compared to what these men must have gone through. The operation was to take place Jan. 30, 1945; the target was a stockade at a place called Cabanatuan, about sixty miles north of Manila.

There were five hundred American prisoners being held there, and in preparation for the assault some Filipino guerillas were to go along the trial and make sure all the local folks had their dogs tied and muzzled, and chickens secured. They didn't want any barking or squawking to alert the Japanese.

I was assigned to a Filipino unit under the command of Lt. Fred Aguisanda. Our job was to blow bridges just north of the camp, to try to block any Japanese reinforcements. We did that once the Rangers and Scouts stormed the gate. Then we got out of there. The raid was one of the great successes of the war, with the prisoners rescued and only a few casualties. I saw the returning POWs. They were so thin you could read a newspaper through them. They were bony and white and wore loose-fitting, dirty shorts and pants that had been frayed to almost nothing.

All of the men had a haunted look about them: cheekbones protruded sharply, their eyes were bulged and unfocused. Some of them were calling, "God bless you all. Thank God for you boys."

IN MARCH 1945 I was given a new assignment — scout for a platoon in Company B of the 152nd Regiment of the 38th Infantry Division. This outfit was operating to the northeast of Manila, an area of rugged jungle uplands, steep hills and rocky ridges. One day the strangest thing happened while on a patrol. We entered a small village that had a lot of rickety frame dwellings in it. It appeared at first that the Japanese had pulled out, but we soon found out that there had been several left behind, just to harass us. Anyway, we were trading shots with them. All of a sudden, a shot comes from the left side of where I'm laying down.

It kicked up dirt and twigs right in front of my face. I turned and saw a Japanese soldier coming out of one of the small shacks, aiming his rifle at me. I rolled around and fired at him. The guy lurched back against the building and fell.

We kept shooting to the front then and after several minutes the other enemy troops were either hit or had run. When it was over we stood up and walked cautiously through the village to make sure it was clear. The platoon leader, Lt. Wilbur Chasteen, from Seymore, Ind., called out, "Hey, Chief, you really nailed this guy."

Chasteen was an earnest young man who seldom joked around. He was standing over the dead soldier who had come out of the house.

"Yeah, I guess I got him," I said.

"Come look at this," he said, pointing at the side of the hut. I walked over to see what he was talking about. Then I saw it. One of the bullets I had fired passed through the Japanese soldier and hit a nail head, embedding itself on it.

WE WERE MOVING inland slowly, pushing the Japanese back. The war, Chasteen said, was being won, although the way he figured it, we might be here for another year or two. I figured it might take five years to win. Chasteen was the first officer I came to know on a personal basis. When we were resting or there was a break in the action, he would talk to me about his plans after the war. And he always talked about a baby his wife gave birth to shortly after he had shipped overseas.

The 38th Division was sent to the high hills that lay along Highway 7, better known to the troops as Zig-Zag Pass because of all the sharp twists and turns in the road. The Japanese held the high ground and would control the road unless we moved into the forests and beat them back.

The Phillipines campaign was more like the war I had envisioned. The Japanese not only held steady defense lines, but they dug tanks into the earth so that just the turret showed above ground.

From these, they had the firepower of a machine gun nest as well as an artillery emplacement.

Lt. Chasteen began calling me by the nickname of "Choo-Choo," because he said I looked like a train when I ran with my cigar puffing smoke into the air. Some of the men called me "Chief," and others "Choo-Choo" Eventually someone, I don't remember who, started calling me "Chooch," which was a combination of the two.

ONE EVENING CHASTEEN and I scouted a partly bald hill that looked like a good place for our planes to drop supplies the next day. We were operating so far from the main road that having planes drop them by parachute was more practical. The only problem was the Japanese watched the parachutes come down, and then made a beeline for the place and tried to pick us off as we collected the goods. We had to be quick.

Once we were re-supplied, we were to move out again and try to break the Japanese grip on the pass. As we waited, Lt. Chasteen talked about home. I listened as I cleaned my Thompson.

Then he said, "Choo-Choo, you got that gun so clean you can almost see your face in it. That's a top-notch job."

"It's not bad," I said. "I like to keep it looking pretty good."

"I've been thinking about getting me one of those," he said.

Then he held up the M-1 rifle he carried. "These damn things are good, but when they get muddy they jam up. You have to use your foot to get the bolt to move. That's not a very fast way to fire."

I laughed. "None of 'em want to fire when they get muddy."

Next morning the planes came over, dropped us more ammunition, water and food, and we picked it up then once again began moving out.

I was walking ahead of the others, the point man, and we were moving through terrain that was mixed tropical trees and grassy hills. After about an hour the word came up to halt. I went back to talk to Chasteen. I had just knelt down beside him when the first shots erupted.

A group of Japanese soldiers trotted toward us, an officer waving a sword in the lead. Chasteen shouted to fire and rolled for cover.

I heard the "thump-thump-thump" sound of his M-1 firing. I grinned. It seemed his weapon was functioning fine. Then I raised the Thompson and squeezed the trigger. Nothing. Not a thing happened. The weapon was jammed. With all the shooting going on, I squatted down near Chasteen and shouted, "I cleaned the damn thing so good it won't fire. It jammed."

He laughed. I kept working the bolt and finally the jam was cleared and I began firing. The Japanese disappeared in the thick growth. To my right, Chasteen rose slightly looking back. I think he was trying to see how many of our guys had been hit. Just then a Japanese machine gun cut loose.

"Down!" I shouted.

But it was too late. Chasteen's body seemed to quiver several times; his face had a strange look of stunned surprise.

"Lieutenant!" I shouted, and rolled toward him. "You all right?"

He didn't answer and I ran to him and got my arms under his back, trying to lift him, to get him out of there. But he was dead weight and I felt the warm, sticky gush of blood on my hands. He didn't say a word and I could tell by the look in his eyes, that distant, vague expression, that he was hit bad. I screamed for a medic.

Then I lowered my voice. "It's going to be all right, sir. We'll get you out of here. It's all right."

His face had a drained, pale look. He tried to say something, but only a hoarse, choking sound came out. Then his eyes rolled back. He died there in my arms with the sound of gunfire rattling in the air around. I wept. It was the only time I shed tears over a comrade in that war.

I sat there for what seemed hours, holding Chasteen in my arms, his blood soaking through to my clothing. And I remembered the words Pearl had spoken to me ages ago. I repeated them to my dead friend. "In war you don't make no plans, because they never work out. They just never work out. You just take what happens."

A medic crawled up and helped me move him to a small clump of trees and rocks. I said a prayer to help send his soul off to heaven, because I knew that's where he was going. I left him then, crawled up the trail and began firing. The war, like time, marched on. I fired my weapon, cursing and reciting the Hail Mary prayer aloud.

It began raining the next morning and I returned to the area where the aid station had been set up. There was still sporadic firing. But the attack had ended. In the light rain Chasteen lay uncovered. Someone had closed his eyes. There was still dirt and dust on his face, but the rain slowly washed it away. We sent Lt. Chasteen to the rear area, lying across the hood of a jeep. I picked up my weapon and went on.

6

Army Rust

In June 1945, the Army issued an order awarding me the Combat Infantryman Badge. The badge goes to an infantry soldier who has performed well in battle. The award is the most coveted a ground soldier can get, although at the time I thought little about it. Some guys, like me, got it for doing all right in combat for thirty days. Others got it for being wounded after only a few days. And some received it by dying within minutes of their first action.

World War II ended for me a few weeks later, in the same general area. It ended with another Japanese attack, followed by our counter attack. A Japanese soldier came busting through the smoke and stopped about fifteen yards away.

I fired a couple of bursts at him, but missed. Then, almost in slow motion, he raised his arm and lightly lobbed a hand grenade at me. I don't think you can accurately describe how you feel when a grenade is tumbling through the air and you know it's going to explode.

My arms had healed on the outside, although they still hurt. But at that moment I didn't think about the pain. I just reached out with my right hand and caught the grenade, then pitched it right back to him.

Well, that soldier's eyes almost popped out. But he just stood there and made a catch himself — it was like we were playing baseball — and he threw it right back to me.

"God Almighty!" I cried.

It only takes a couple of seconds for an activated grenade to blow. I was going to try to catch it again and hurriedly throw it back at him. But time ran out on me. The thing went off in mid-air, about three or four yards from me.

I was aware of the blast and felt my face burning. Then I went out. When I regained consciousness I apparently was at an aid station, because I could hear our medics talking. But I couldn't see a thing. The explosion had damaged my eyes. I was afraid I'd be blind for life, but a doctor later told me I would regain my vision. And then he added somewhat hesitantly, "Probably. There are no guarantees."

There never are in war.

I was put on a ship and a month later I was at the Oakland Army Hospital. My vision began to return, although I was seeing blurry for weeks. While there the doctors did some maintenance work on my arms, and inserted some wire to help support the bones and muscles which had been damaged by the Japanese guy and his bayonet. I was at the hospital when the news came about the atomic bomb and, a few days later, the Japanese surrender.

I WAS DISCHARGED from the Army in March 1946 and went home to Boston, a civilian again. Because of my wounds, I was awarded a partial disability by the Veterans Administration, and given what was known as the "52/20" ride, meaning they'd pay me $20 a week for 52 weeks, enough time for me to be able to get back on my feet with a job. My arms weren't in good shape because of the bayonet wounds, but my legs were as good as ever, maybe even a little stronger. I figured I could work at something and make a good living, along with the VA money I was going to get.

America's economy was booming because of construction. New homes would be needed for all the GIs coming home. They would be getting married and raising families . . . most of them, not me, though. I found a job in Boston with a construction outfit that was putting up buildings. The foreman was a big, ugly guy about forty or so, a beer drinker who had no great respect for combat infantry veterans. One day I dropped a hot bolt from a beam about thirteen stories up and he saw it.

He looks up and hollers, "Get your fat ass down here."

I came down and looked him in the eye. "You talking to me?"

"Yeah, I'm talking to you," he said.

Already in trouble, I figured I might as well get a little sarcastic. "I thought maybe you were talking to yourself, because you've got the fattest ass around here."

"You're fired," he said, his face red. "Go to the cage and pick up your pay and get the hell off my property."

I laughed in his face. "What, no going-away party?"

He turned away then. So I said nothing more and left, ending my brief career in the construction business. When a guy comes home from a war there's always some so-called "Army rust" on him, an attitude that's harder for some to shake than others. You had to do your best to try to fit back into normal society.

Fitting in meant having some money, which I desperately needed. So I went to the boxing arena and signed on. I felt I could get my arms in shape to fight. For the next year that's what I did, fighting once a week, sometimes twice, getting twenty dollars each time. Some I won, some I lost, and it was painful each time. My arms were not up to the demands of boxing, but there was no quitting.

I was trying to to be a model citizen. But my father, when he heard about the disability pay, was unhappy with me. He got home one day and I went to visit.

"How was it in the Pacific?" he asked.

I shrugged. "Kind of rough, Dad. But I guess you know that. War is war."

He sort of laughed and looked away. "You have to deal with it." Then he said, "What's this about disability?"

"What do you mean?" I was defensive. "I got a partial. I'm not the only one."

But he shook his head and turned away and went into another room. I stared at him. My father was never going to be satisfied with my life, I thought.

One day I got a letter from the VA asking me to come in for a review of my status. When I got there some clerical guy behind a desk fidgeted through my papers, then said: "We hear you've been boxing."

"A little," I said cautiously. "Now and then."

"If you're well enough to box," he said, "then there's no need for you to be considered disabled."

Within a week I received notice that I had been removed from the 52/20 plan. I would now have to depend entirely on boxing to try to survive. It was barely enough to pay my rent, much less afford a date a couple of times a week. I dated several different girls, but none was serious.

It was difficult for me to adjust to civilian life. After more than five years in the Army, I couldn't stand for people to push and shove in stores, or get ahead of me in the popcorn line at a movie theater. Some nights I would dream about the war, and often would wake up and swear I heard gunfire. Even awake, I would find my thoughts drifting back to New Guinea or the Philippines.

One night I dreamed about two black soldiers who had been hanged in New Guinea after being found guilty of raping a white nurse. It had happened in October 1944, ten minutes after two o'clock on a Sunday afternoon. I would never forget. I had to help build the thirteen steps to the gallows. Oh, hell yeah, I was right there. The guy that did the hanging was a big old master sergeant. Years later, the sergeant committed suicide at Fort Leavenworth, Kansas. He killed himself by hanging.

PART TWO

KOREA

7

A Soldier Again

I DECIDED THE only life I could succeed at was the military one, but in 1947 the Army was downgrading from World War II. Things were just starting to get edgy with the Russians over Berlin.

I went to a local recruiting station and thought they'd sign me up in a heartbeat since I was a combat veteran. But the wounds I had sustained made me a poor candidate, at least as far as the recruiting sergeant was concerned. So I decided to pull some strings. I called my father who had contacts in the Pentagon. He called me back a couple of hours later and told me to report in two days to a Maj. Gen. Edward F. Witsell at the Pentagon. He was the Army's adjutant general.

"I told him about you and asked him to help," my father said. "He didn't make any promises. But he agreed to see you. So it's up to you. I went out on a limb for you. Look sharp. Wear a coat and tie."

"I'll do it." Then I added, "Thanks a lot, Dad."

He laughed. "OK. I wouldn't do this for just anyone. Don't let me down."

"Don't worry."

Hanging up the telephone, I shook my head. I had been through a war but still wasn't the soldier my father had hoped for. That had to be changed. I hurriedly packed my bags and went to the train station. I couldn't afford to show up late for this appointment.

Until that moment it never occurred to me that I might make a career of the Army. During the war I kept my mind on the business at hand, and thought only vaguely about civilian life. I hadn't really thought much about my future. In fact, I had begun to live by the words that were a guide until that time, the words Pearl had spoken: "Don't make plans. They never work out."

It was a Thursday when I got to Washington. It was raining; I felt uncomfortable in the tight-fitting brown suit. I caught a cab to the Pentagon, then located Gen. Witsell's office. A secretary told me to have a seat in the waiting room. About twenty minutes later I was summoned. I started to salute, but remembered I was still a civilian. He glanced up at me.

"So you're Sergeant Pinn's boy," he said. "You look like him."

"Yes, sir."

He hadn't invited me to sit, so I stood at attention, waiting.

"You know we don't have a lot of room anymore," the general said rather grumpily. "We damn sure don't need any trouble-makers."

"Sir?"

"I saw your record," he snorted with contempt. "Disorderly conduct and fighting."

"Yes, sir, but I did OK in the war, sir."

"Well, we're not in a war now, mister," he said. "At least not yet."

The general stood up then and paced about the office, apparently thinking about his decision.

Still at attention, I said, "Sir, if I could get back in I know I'd do a better job. And I think I could be of help in training the new guys coming along."

He didn't say a word then, just stood staring at me for a moment. Then, he said, "Well, I hope so. For your sake and mine. And for your father's. He's one hell of a good soldier."

"Yes, sir."

"All right, then." And with that the general went back to his desk, picked up some papers and glanced up at me. "We'll let you back in, but I want you to know you'll go back as a private-first class, not a sergeant. Is that understood?"

"Yes, sir. I appreciate it."

The general nodded. "If you're half the man your father is, you'll soon be back up to sergeant."

"Yes, sir. Thank you, sir. I appreciate the opportunity."

He told me he'd send me my orders in a few days. I went back to Boston and within a week the paperwork came through and I reported to the recruiting station. I was back in the Army.

THE FIRST THING I wanted to try was the airborne, to hook up a parachute and leap out of a plane. It sounded like the thrill of a lifetime. But on my physical training test I had a difficult time doing the pull-ups and the push-ups that were required to pass the airborne's tough standards. I could have run with them for miles, but the injuries to the arms from the Japanese soldier's bayonet had left an impact.

My first assignment was a refresher course where I ended up helping instruct trainees on the bayonet. I also became involved in the physical training. It helped me get back into fairly good shape. Then they sent me to the headquarters for the Sixth Army, which was located at the Presidio, near Monterey, California. It was also near Fort Ord, where I had trained before being sent to the Southwest Pacific. After a few months of taking a course in Army administration, I was assigned as an aide to Gen. Mark Clark, who had commanded the Fifth Army in Italy. Clark seemed to like me all right and I was soon made a corporal, and before long I was back to sergeant.

The general was a Citadel graduate, and would later return there as president. One day this beautiful young lady strolls into the office and I asked her if I could be of assistance.

"The general's my daddy," she said and breezed by my desk and into his office. Later, she came out with him and the general introduced us.

"You know," said Clark, putting an arm around her, "I wouldn't mind if you married Sergeant Pinn, honey. He's a good guy. But he's got one drawback."

"Really? What's that?"

She took the words right out of my mouth. "He didn't graduate from the Citadel."

Clark grinned.

I laughed. "Well, maybe it's not too late to enroll."

It was good duty at Clark's headquarters, but it was getting me soft. So I took up boxing again, fighting in the military ranks. I beat some of the Army's best, as well as the Navy's. And I got beat some. In one bout I was knocked down twice in one round, and I heard the referee counting me out. He had reached five and I figured I'd just stay down and let it end.

But then I heard a major shouting at me, "Pinn, get your butt up and fight."

Through the sweat that blurred my vision I saw the major . . . but my eyes locked on a young woman who was sitting beside him. I don't know who she was, but she was beautiful. I couldn't lay there and let her see me get whipped. So I got on my feet, wobbled a bit, and waited. My opponent thought he had me, and charged forward to finish me off. I side-stepped, then threw a right that had everything left in me.

It landed right on his chin, and I could see his eyes go sort of dazed looking, then I came over with a left cross, then another right. Next thing I knew, he was down and out. I won that fight because of the girl. I never did know who she was.

But boxing wasn't enough, and I had enough of office work. I became restless. I still wanted to go airborne. General Clark patiently listened to my pleading that I was a soldier and felt I would do better if I was assigned to a good infantry division. Finally he agreed to let me go, joking to the last that if I had gone to the Citidel, he would consider me as a possible future son-in-law.

I was assigned to the 2nd Infantry Division at Fort Lewis, Washington, becoming the sergeant of the R&I platoon of the 38th Regiment. R&I is for Reconnaisance and Intelligence, or Recon for short. The job is to probe out ahead of the rest of the regiment and see what an enemy is doing as well as try to get prisoners. We did some tough training preparing for combat. We didn't know how close at hand it was.

8

A New Love and a New War

IN LATE 1949 I met an Alabama girl, Una Norris; I fell in love with her. We married in January 1950. It was the year of a new love. It would also be the year of a new war.

It started on June 25, 1950, in a place called Korea, a Far East country most Americans had never heard of. Communist North Korea invaded South Korea, which was a democracy, supported by the U.S.

Una and I had gone out to eat dinner that night when we heard some of the people at the restaurant talking about the invasion. It didn't seem like it could be a big war, but I wondered about it. The next morning I reported for duty and was told that we had been placed on alert for possible shipment. President Truman had already committed American aircraft to help the South Koreans who were in steady retreat.

The North Koreans had stormed across the dividing line — the 38th Parallel — and were moving south. Their Russian-made tanks led the assault, which was cutting the South Korean Army to pieces. In early July Truman ordered ground troops to be sent in to assist. The Far East Command sent 540 troops from the 24th Infantry Division, based in Japan, flying them in. Within a day they were in action and being ripped by the Reds. The 24th troops had been given an impossible task. They were green, under-equipped, and too few in number. The retreat would be the first of many.

The 2nd Division was ordered to Korea. We quickly packed, tied up loose ends, then held a hastily organized farewell parade. The band played El Capitan as we strode by the reviewing stand. The people in the bleachers cheered. Then we boarded ships and headed for the strange new war. The boat ride over was much faster than the World War II trip. In about eighteen days we arrived in Pusan, the port city on the southeast coast.

Korea is shaped like Florida in a way, a peninsula jutting from the Asian mainland. The Sea of Japan is on the eastern side, the Yellow Sea on the west. To the north is Manchuria with its trackless plains and wind-swept mountains, a land controlled by the Red Chinese, the largest army in the world.

We arrived in early August, and by then three American divisions were fighting for their lives in what came to be known as the Pusan Perimeter. It was a defensive line about forty miles around the port. The 24th and 25th Infantry Divisions, plus the 1st Cavalry Division (an infantry division that we warmly referred to as "horseshit and gunsmoke") had managed to cling to the position until help came. We debarked at about the same time the 1st Marine Division arrived.

One of the first things that struck me was the smell of the place. There were thousands of people crammed in the city, refugees from the war. As we were marched to an assembly point, we passed acres of rice paddies, which were fertilized with human excrement. In the rising mist of hot mornings, the aroma can be a bit overpowering.

We loaded onto trucks for a lift to the frontline area. It began raining as we bumped along over the muddy roads, finally coming to a halt about twenty-five miles west of Pusan. Then we began walking. By then we could hear the sound of artillery firing. Once an American P-51 fighter screamed low as it made a turn, then headed back to the northwest to make a strafing run. The war was getting closer. We stopped at the base of a high hill and were told to stack our gear. In the the distance the rumble of artillery and the thump of mortars being fired grew louder, peppered with rifle and machine gun fire.

"Sounds like old times doesn't it, Sarge?" asked Cpl. Ed Leeming, my best friend in the platoon. I eased my gear off the truck, then nodded at him. "Yeah, sort of like old times."

Leeming was from Narragansett, Rhode Island. I noted that his voice was a little edgy, which was understandable. Then something struck me. This was a new war. I was not the kid anymore. At age 28, I was the old veteran, the sergeant in charge. I saw the anxious expressions on the young faces.

"All right, men," I said, taking time to light a cigar. "Now we're going to be going up on the line pretty soon. Just remember what you were taught and you'll be all right. Don't do nothing foolish. Main thing is I don't want anyone getting killed."

The platoon leader, Lt. Ben Gibbons, arrived a moment later from a hurried staff meeting, and signaled for me to follow him. We were to dig in on the northwest end of the hill and prepare for a North Korean attack, Gibbons told me. We were to help stabilize the line around Pusan, and then later would take up our duties to seek information and take prisoners. For the time being we didn't have to look for the enemy. He was looking for us.

9

On the Naktong

THAT NIGHT THE North Koreans dropped some mortars around our positions, and several enemy troops crawled close enough to lob grenades and fire submachine guns at us, then fled. Gibbons fired a flare and in the lurid, whitish-blue light I saw several of them running. I fired but missed, and to my left Leeming and Pfc. Johnny Coyle unloaded their M-1s.

"Let's keep heads up," I said, after the firing stopped. "These guys are pretty good."

My God, I thought, they had to be good . . . better than I thought they might be. Here they were keeping the American Army on its heels. I put another magazine into the Tommy gun, watched for a time, then crawled along the line making sure everyone was all right. One of the guys asked me, "Is this going to go on all night?"

"Don't know," I said. "But it might. They have to sleep, too."

We had two guys in each hole, so I had one sleep while the other kept watch. The holes were about ten yards apart, close enough for the men to keep in visual contact. We didn't have any dead or wounded, but some of the other units of the regiment farther along the perimeter took the first casualties to be suffered by the 2nd Division. There would be many more.

The next day we got our first good look at the North Korean troops. They wore mustard yellow uniforms, soft caps, and most carried Russian-made burp guns and rifles. They attacked the position we held with a frontal assault, running up the hillside. We first saw them coming across the valley, running single file in a ravine, then spreading out as they came up the hill.

My guys went quiet.

"On your toes," I said. "Wait till you get the word before you fire. Remember, there's no place to run."

On came the North Koreans. At first they shouted, then they started throwing grenades, a futile effort because they were too far away. The things started rolling back down the hill and exploding. But then they started firing just as their mortar support fire came in.

The terrain was rugged; the hills were ribbed with wide, deep gullies, and finger-like rises that ran parallel, giving the attackers cover as they came up. I found it frustrating because in order to fire downhill I had to rise up out of the foxhole and expose most of the upper half of my body.

The North Koreans could go flat, then fire along the upslope; the bullets would hug the lay of the land, hitting right at chest level. We finally threw the attack back, but after that we revised our firing pattern. We would avoid firing directly in front and downhill, but rather we would use crossing patterns. That would lessen the risk of making ourselves good targets.

After several weeks on the line, the men began to adapt to being combat infantrymen. They didn't light cigarettes at night, unless in a well-covered foxhole; they learned to trust their instinct at night, believing in what they saw. There was less firing at non-existent targets, although from time to time things got so edgy that there were spontaneous outbursts of rifle and machine gun fire. We weren't the only ones. Sometimes while trying to sleep I'd hear distant firing, and look up into the night sky to the east or west and see tracers bouncing around into the darkness. A flare would glow eerily, hanging like a dying star. Then it would go quiet.

We were on line in the southwest section of the perimeter, located near the Marines. But we rarely stayed in one place long, as Maj. Gen. Laurence Keiser kept getting orders pulling us out of the line and trucking us somewhere else to fill in a breach in the defense.

Keiser was a World War I vet and had also been in World War II. This was his third war. But he still preferred the Springfield bolt-action rifle, which he carried with him when he came up to the front.

EARLY IN SEPTEMBER we began taking out patrols, looking for signs of enemy activity and trying to grab a prisoner or two. It meant coming down out of the hills and getting on the flat country, following narrow roads and paths. About ten uf us were going. I was getting the men checked out and Lt. Gibbons gave us one final rundown. Then Gibbons turned to Ed Leeming.

"Soldier, you just volunteered for the point," he said.

For some reason the lieutenant had a grudge against Leeming, who was my closest buddy. I didn't know why, but it put me in a fix. I preferred to share the burden of being the point man. The point means you're the front guy. But Leeming just smiled at Gibbons and shrugged, saying, "Yes, sir. I got the point."

As we moved along down into the valley Coyle called, "Ed, you know the first one to get shot at is the point guy."

But Leeming laughed. "Not here," he said. "These guys let

you go by them then they turn and get you in the back. The last guy's the one to get it."

He had a point. The thing about Korea was that many North Korean soldiers dressed in white clothing, the same as the peasants who worked the rice paddies. Under the loose-fitting garments, they could easily hide a Russian-made burp gun or grenades. We never knew who the enemy might be for sure. There were cases where women had fired upon our troops.

On this day we came upon a village which, at first glance, seemed quiet, even deserted. I moved up beside Leeming and looked the place over through binoculars.

"Anything?" he asked.

I saw a few people in white working in a field beyond the first small hut.

About that time I heard a bullet whizzing by and shouted, "Down!" but it was not necessary. The men had already flattened into the ditches on either side of the road.

The shot was followed by several more. They had come from the second hut, or as some of the men called them, the hooch. We spread out and flanked the place, firing as we did so. A couple of guys in white pajama-like outfits ran out and we fired.

One of them fell flat dead, the other sort of jumped into the air then crumbled down along the edge of the ditch. We searched the other huts as the field workers shouted excitedly at us, telling us, I think, that there were no more North Koreans around.

The next day, another patrol ran into more fire from the village. The orders came down the line for us to send another patrol and this time I was to carry explosives. We cleared the area, made sure there were no civilians around, then set small charges in the small floor fireplaces which heated the quarters in winter. Then we blew them up.

As the charges went off, an old woman and a little girl stood on the road beside us, wailing and moaning, pleading with us not to destroy their homes. The old lady grabbed at my arm.

I shook my head and patted her on the shoulder. "We have to do it," I told her. Then I pointed to the southeast, toward Pusan.

"Chogi," I said. The word, as I understood it, meant a trail or path, to move out smartly, or as Americans are known to say, "haul ass." Korea was a dirty war. In many ways, it was like Vietnam would later become. In July, while the 2nd Infantry was still on the high seas, some of the boys from the 1st Cavalry had been captured. The North Koreans bound their wrists with wire, then shot them. There were other atrocities. We didn't want to destroy villages, but we had to take away hiding places from the North Koreans.

One night Gibbons passed along a new order from higher command: we were to allow Koreans in civilian clothing, presumably refugees, to pass through our lines during the days. But at night, we were ordered to fire on them. There had been too many incidents of our men being shot by North Koreans dressed in civilian attire.

THE NORTH KOREANS were getting desparate to crack our lines and wedge us into the sea. But each day we received more reinforcements, while the North Koreans began to exhaust their supplies. They turned more to night attacks.

We were down on the banks of the Naktong River one night when they came across again, and the fire fight went on for more than an hour. Then, with most of us out of ammunition, it turned into a scrimmage.

One of our guys had been hit and left his M-1 nearby. I fired out what was in the weapon, then used the bayonet.

It was a nightmare come true: There were men cursing, shouting, and running in all directions . . . smoke hanging in a thick cloud . . . flares going off, a lurid bluish-white, sputtering above . . . men sweating and heaving for breath . . . isolated shots going off or a grenade exploding . . . helmets rolling crazily about . . . a man on his hands and knees crawling wobbily in a circle, then falling and laying still . . . and the strange popping sound that came when a rifle butt made contact with a skull.

A North Korean soldier in a white shirt popped up in front of me and snarled some battle cry, then lunged. I sidestepped him and butted him pretty good in the chest, knocking him down. But I didn't get away from another one who came in from the side. He yelled, I turned, and—CRACK!—something hit me right in the mouth. I saw stars and felt a sharp pain just explode through my head. I went down. Was it a shot or a rifle butt? I didn't know. But I was down, and helpless.

"God, I'm getting killed," I said to myself.

I tasted blood — a lot of blood—then looked up in a daze as the North Korean stood above me, ready to finish me off. I watched paralyzed as he prepared to plunge the bayonet into my gut. But it seemed like he froze, and then —God Almighty!—he just crumpled. I let out a weak shout. Then, my head throbbing, I managed to get up and stand wobbily, looking about me. I could see the fight, but could do nothing to help out. I finally concluded that somebody had shot the guy who was going to kill me. I looked down at him and saw blood coming from a hole in his head. Apparently, not everyone had run out of ammo. Groggily, I staggered around, feeling worse than I'd ever felt in a boxing match. The night ended with the North Koreans running back across the river.

A medic gave me a shot of morphine and told me I had taken a solid whack from a rifle butt. I went to sleep. Next morning I got up to a terrible headache. My face was swollen and my mouth felt strange. The North Korean's rifle butt had taken out most of my front teeth.

Lt. Gibbons came up and asked, "You all right, Sergeant?"

I nodded. "Damn fine, sir."

He nodded. "Well, it's probably going to be hard to chomp on those big cigars."

I nodded. "I'll manage, sir."

IN EARLY SEPTEMBER MacArthur ordered the 1st Marine Division off the line and hurriedly sent them to the rear, where they loaded onto boats and sailed up the west coast. On September 15 they made a surprise landing at Inchon, a port city about 25 miles west of Seoul, then captured the South Korean capital. Within a few days we were moving north, routing the North Korean Army before us. Some of our units were getting on trucks and racing up the narrow roads, things were going so fast. By October, we were crossing the 38th Parallel into North Korea.

Everyone was talking about the war being over soon, that we would be heading back to either Japan or the U.S. We were told that Red China was threatening to enter the war if we crossed into North Korea. But Gen. MacArthur issued reports that the Red Chinese would stay out, and if they did enter, we would chop them up.

Now, the staff officers at 38th Regimental headquarters were pushing us to get prisoners. The days were getting cool, the nights brisk. This part of Korea was similar in climate to Ohio or Michigan. There were high hills all around and far to the east was the towering Taebaek Range. It was so high and rugged that it separated the U.S. Eighth Army, of which we were a part, from X Corps, which was on the east side of the peninsula. There were few roads or paths across the range.

One day we captured a couple of kids who were in North Korean uniform and I questioned them, using an interpreter. An Army photographer snapped a picture of it and the shot ended up in Newsweek magazine. There I was trying to chomp on a cigar with most of my teeth missing. I sent a note home to Una telling her about the kids, but adding, "They can kill as well as a grown man if they have a gun in their hands."

When North Korea first invaded, it had an army of about 200,000 troops, but after the breakout from Pusan and our pursuit across the 38th Parallel, their ranks dropped to about 50,000, scattered across the country; many deserted or gave up. As we stepped up our patrols, the two things we were looking for were 1) any sign of troops from Red China entering the war, and 2) some idea of how much of an army the North Koreans retained. One bright cool afternoon Leeming and Coyle and I entered a village, which was quiet and without any sign of life. The rest of the patrol stayed back about a hundred yards, keeping us covered. I heard someone talking in Korean and called out a warning.

There was no response, but the talk continued. Finally I approached the hut and nudged the door open with my foot. Inside I saw several wounded North Koreans laying on the floor, They were being treated by three young women who wore medical emblems on their sleeves.

"Nurses," Leeming said, looking over my shoulder. "What do we do?"

I shrugged. "Take 'em back with us."

The North Korean nurses did not appear to be afraid of us, and kept their focus on the wounded. They nodded solemnly when we told them we were taking them with us. I signaled for the other men to come up and we carried the wounded back to our lines, turning the medical people over to our intelligence unit.

Later that day I was sitting in a jeep smoking a cigar when I saw Col. George Peploe, the commanding officer of the 38th, walking hurriedly along the road toward me. Lt. Gibbons hurried up to join him. It wasn't often the regimental commander came up to our platoon for a visit.

Peploe looked right at me. "Pinn, I want prisoners."

"Yes, sir," I said, standing up and glancing at Gibbons.

"I'm tired of kids and nurses," the colonel went on. "Get out there and get some real North Korean soldiers. We need to know what's up ahead of us."

He turned abruptly and left, hardly noting the presence of Lt. Gibbons. It was me he was after. I looked at Leeming and Coyle. Then I turned to the lieutenant, "I guess we'll go back out again in the morning."

Gibbons raised his eyebrows. "I do believe that's a good idea." Then he grinned, adding, "And damn it, Sergeant Pinn, get us some prisoners."

NEXT DAY WE went out again. We were tired but there was a feeling of near-euphoria among most of us that we were going to wrap this thing up quickly and it would be over. As we walked along a narrow dirt road some of the men talked about spending Christmas in Japan.

We passed through the village where we had taken the nurses and moved on another mile or so. A South Korean soldier was with us to act as interpreter. I called him Hong.

Overhead a jet roared eastward, and off in the distance there was the sound of small arms fire. Otherwise, the morning was quiet. Ahead of us was a small rise that lay beyond a field of yellowed corn stalks. We studied the place for a time, saw nothing, then began to move again over the road that lay alongside the cornfield.

About that time a Korean man came running down the road, and some of the men raised their weapons.

"Hold it," I said. "Just get down."

I didn't have to tell them, they were already squatting in the ditches, watching. The man stopped about twenty yards from us and began talking excitedly, pointing back toward the rise.

"He says there are enemy soldiers behind the ridge," Hong said.

Just as he finished speaking a shot rang out from ahead. We went flat. I looked up, but saw nothing.

"Where'd that hit?" I called. "Anyone hear it?"

No one answered. I looked back down the line. The men shook their heads. "Somebody's got bad aim," I said. "Or else they didn't want to hit us."

We stayed down for another minute or so while we watched the rise. The Korean man, who appeared to be in his forties or so, maybe a farmer, also squatted down on the road, waiting. It seemed to me that the North Koreans on the other side of the rise were not in a mood to fight. Maybe they were waiting to surrender. Or maybe it was a trap. But there was no sense waiting all day.

I tapped Hong on the shoulder. "Come on, I want to go up the road and you tell them we have food and will treat them fairly if they surrender," I said.

"Hold it, Sarge," Leeming called. "Might be a trap. Don't go up there."

But I got up and began walking along the road toward the rise. Hong stayed a few paces to the rear. Behind me I heard

Leeming calling to the others, "That crazy Indian is going up there. Get ready to cover."

We drew nearer to the rise and I muttered to Hong, "Tell 'em what I said."

Hong shouted out the message in Korean. There was no response. Then, in the distance we heard someone call out.

Hong looked at me. "He wants to be sure you won't shoot them. He says they were told Americans kill their own mothers."

"Tell them, no, that's a lie," I said. "Tell them we have food and warm clothing and beds for them to sleep in. Tell them when the war is over we can let them go home to their families. Tell them our mothers are sacred."

He called out again, speaking in rapid-fire fashion. For a moment there was nothing, then we saw some movement. Two or three young North Koreans cautiously emerged, holding their rifles high.

I kept my Tommy gun pointed down at the ground. "Tell the others to come out," I said to Hong. "Make it sound polite."

Now several others followed the first group; they put their weapons on the ground, raised their hands on their heads, and stepped forward a few feet. Then I turned and began walking slowly back down the narrow road.

"Tell the others to come out and put down their weapons and follow me, that I will take them to the hot food," I said.

He relayed the message. After a few moments I heard the sound of many feet crushing through the dead plants and leaves that were drying in the autumn sunshine. They walked in silence for a time, then came onto the road, and began chattering. I heard the sounds of the weapons hitting the ground. By now I was walking through my patrol, my men in a state of quiet surprise, holding their weapons pointed up at the port arms position.

"Just play it cool," I said. "After we search them, let them pass by, then go up and collect their weapons and fall in."

The North Koreans now formed a double column. There must have been forty or fifty of them, although it looked at first like several hundred. They followed us down the road to our lines; when we got there Lt. Gibbons came out and stood with hands on his hips.

"You can tell Colonel Peploe that we got him some prisoners," I told him.

The field mess tent fixed some rice and cabbage for the prisoners. I never did hear anything from Peploe. As we sat down for a meal of chipped beef and coffee, I heard some of the men talking about our patrol, and mentioning "that crazy Indian," meaning me. I did what I did because I felt the North Koreans were prepared to give up. If I hadn't thought that, I would not have walked out in the open. There is a place for bravery in this man's Army. But there is no place for being a fool.

10

Snow . . . and Chinese Everywhere

By middle October the 1st Cavalry took Pyongyang, the North Korean capital, and all UN forces kept rolling northward. Late in the month we were in the bleak hill country about forty miles from the Yalu River, which is the boundary between North Korea and Manchuria. The nights were getting cold and there were gray, gloomy days when snow flurries swirled over us as we carried out patrols. There was talk of some of us getting some time off to maybe go to Toyko or at least back to Seoul, but it was mostly talk. We did manage to get a few days off so we could shower, sleep in a tent, and get a haircut.

But then on November 1 the word came to mount up and be ready to move out, that something had gone wrong. The 8th Regiment of the 1st Cav had been ambushed near Unsan, to the northwest of us, and had been badly mauled. It was scary talk. Cav men had been bayoneted as they slept in their sleeping bags. Their attackers were not the North Koreans, but Chinese troops.

Then a strange thing happened. After the attack, the Chinese seemed to disappear in the bleak hills that tumbled into the vast wastelands of Manchuria. We were told to pull back and regroup along the Chongchon River, about fifty miles or so from the Yalu River. Gen. MacArthur, who had so confidently sent us across North Korea, was showing some concern about Chinese intentions.

It was an uneasy time for a soldier in Korea. If China entered the war we would not be going home for Christmas and some would never leave Korea alive. The ideas of Chinese coming into the war seemed to paralyze the South Korean troops, who were on our right. The days were not only cold, but anxious as we wondered if the Chinese might strike again. All the cheerful talk of victory by the holiday season was replaced by a kind of sadness as the men talked about home. I received a letter from Una, who sent me a clipping from a newspaper about the college football season.

Princeton had defeated Penn in one of the big games, and was ranked No. 1 in the country. We were sitting alongside a frozen road as I re-read the letter and the clips. Princeton still had to play Yale and Harvard, but as always, the really big game was going to be Harvard and Yale.

"Hey, Leeming," I called. "You got it made here, you know."

He grinned. "How's that?"

"You could be stuck at the Yale Bowl watching the Harvard game," I said. "They tell me it gets colder than hell there."

He laughed. "I just never realized how lucky we are."

By mid-November the Chinese seemed to have vanished from the face of the Earth. There were tons of turkey flown into Korea and we were told we'd have an old-fashioned American feast on Thanksgiving, November 23. At the same time, there were plans afoot for a new offensive that Gen. MacArthur said would end the war, driving the North Korean Army, or what was left of it, across the Yalu River and out of Korea. Our lines were roughly along the Chongchon River, with some of the regiments north of it, others just to the south. The 2nd Division headquarters was located in the crossroads village of Kunu-ri.

A few days before the holiday I took a patrol up a dirt road heading north, crossed the river, then climbed aboard a truck which took us several miles. It stopped when someone with a rifle opened fire. We disembarked then moved several miles without hearing anything more.

It was early afternoon when we took a break, posting lookouts on the flanks. The men ate rations and smoked cigarettes. I had a cigar. I never let the men smoke when we were scouting for enemy positions, because tobacco can be smelled for some distance. I told them, "If you're going to smoke, do it now."

After a few minutes rest I called Leeming over to me. "You take charge," I told him. "I'm going up on that hill to see if there's anything going up ahead."

"Where you going?" he asked.

"Up on that hill."

"Don't forget your way back."

It was kind of an eerie place to be . . . desolate and cold, the only sound the rasp of browned corn stalks rattling in the wind. I had an uneasy feeling that we were probably being watched. For a moment I looked at the hill and thought of the words of Grandfather Joe Charles, who taught me to trust my instincts.

I slapped Leeming on the shoulder. "Hang loose. I'll be back in a flash."

The frozen earth gave way under my feet, making a loud crunching sound. It took fifteen minutes of hard climbing to get to the hilltop. My breath was coming in short gasps and my chest was pounding. Running up a hill in frozen Korea was a little bit tougher than running a marathon. I got out my binoculars and looked over the terrain. There was a river almost directly ahead of me. It didn't show up on any map I'd seen, but that didn't surprise me. Our maps seldom showed rivers, and often noted roads that did not, in fact, exist. I thought we might be near the Yalu, but not this close.

Then I saw the damnest thing. There were Chinese troops coming across the river; some were on horses, some on camels. The sight almost put me in a trance; it was like looking at something from the days of Genghis Khan: an Asiatic army sweeping out of the Middle Ages and crossing into the present.

"Holy hell," I muttered. As I watched, other Chinese soldiers seemed to rise up out of the ground on the northern bank of the river, then ride the animals across. They wore thick-padded uniforms and fur caps. Once on the south side, they moved to a ravine that cut into the base of the long slope that fell away from the knob on which I was standing.

It was time to deploy out of there. I quickly ran down the hillside, crouching low. If they saw us, we were going to be in a lot of trouble, or as British Gen. Montgomery might have said, "in a rather awkward situation."

The men were on their feet when they saw me, apparently alarmed by my haste. I was waving at them, pointing south. When I got closer I called in a low voice, "To the rear, march! Fast as hell."

"What's wrong?" someone asked.

"Chinese," I said. "The world's full of Chinese. They're riding camels."

We moved back at double time until we reached the trucks. Then we headed back to our lines as quickly as possible. Ordinarily I would have radioed a report back once we got in range, but in Korea the PRC-10 radio, which we had, seldom worked well at any distance. The numerous hills blocked it. So Lt. Gibbons, who never smiled much anyway, gazed somberly to the north as I told him about the Chinese.

"Lionel," he said, without looking at me, "I wish I hadn't heard that. We're probably going to be stuck here forever."

He relayed my report to 38th Regiment headquarters. Col. Peploe sent word for me to report to him on the double. I lit a cigar and walked to the HQ tent.

"What's this about camels, Pinn?" he asked.

"Camels, sir," I said. "Chinese on camels."

There was another colonel there, Paul Freeman, who commanded the 23rd Regiment. He regarded me with an amiable grin. He made a comment to the effect that we need not worry about Chinese on camels.

It occurred to me that he didn't believe it. Peploe stared at me for a moment, then nodded and said, "OK, Sergeant Pinn. Go get some food and some rest."

I saluted and went back to the platoon. Outside the air was turning colder, and sleet and jelly-like drops of nearly frozen rain fell. We had a tent with a kerosene stove in it, a place to get warm and even take a nap if you were off duty. There was coffee brewing. I got a cup and sipped it. Then I slept through the night.

Next morning the world was still in one piece. Then Thanksgiving came. It dried out for a day. By the time I got my turkey and sweet potato pie, it was almost cold, but I devoured it anyway, my thoughts on Una and home. Una liked sweet potato pie, but she was from Alabama where it was more of a favorite. I still preferred pumpkin.

For some reason, I never did know why, Leeming had been sent up on a mission toward the north and somehow managed to miss his Thanksgiving dinner. When he got back later that afternoon, all that was left was some canned beans and franks.

"This is one Thanksgiving I'll never forget," he said gloomily.

LIKE ALL INFANTRY divisions in Korea, the 2nd contained about 17,500 men. There were three regiments of about 3,000 men each. The rest of the division was made up of artillery, tank units, medical, supply and so on.

On November 24 MacArthur's "offensive to end the war" began, with all units moving cautiously northward. My regiment, the 38th, was on the right flank; the 9th Regiment was on the left and to the north of the river; the 23rd was in reserve, but moving up to pass through us. That way we sort of leap-frogged along. The first day was mostly a march up rugged hillsides in cold weather, with some snow falling. We set up perimeters that night, then resumed the drive the next morning, November 25. Late in the afternoon we set up camp in a valley. To the west was a hill known as Chinaman's Hat, called that because of the shape of its three peaks. At the time I don't believe anyone in the entire Eighth Army appreciated the irony of the name.

To the west two miles or so were units of the 9th Regiment; just to the west was the 23rd, and just to the north, maybe a half mile, was the 61st Artillery Battalion, which normally was assigned to the 1st Cavalry. As we had supper that evening, we heard firing and saw tracers and flares. The reports had come back through the day that Chinese troops were engaging elements of the 9th at a hill across the Chongchon.

Night fell, the moon rose, and the landscape was lit up as the beams glistened on the layer of snow. The firing continued and Lt. Gibbons told us to stay loose. It would be the last warm night we would spend in a long time. We had some tents set up with a kerosene stove giving warmth, and most of us sat near it as we ate canned hash and drank coffee. Then we heard bugles blowing in the distance. The sound of firing increased and sounded nearer.

I rolled to my feet picking up the Tommy gun. "Come on, get ready. We're going to be in a free-for-all."

Just then we heard a disturbance, the sound of men shouting and running, and I ducked outside. A flare popped and lit up the night, revealing a scene that looked like a bad dream. In the distance we saw American troops running southward. They were being chased by Chinese soldiers. I hurried into the headquarters tent and the scene there was chaos: everyone was talking at the same time.

The gist of it was that there was a general attack all along the front by large numbers of Chinese troops. To the west the 9th was in trouble as was the 25th Division. To the east, on our immediate right flank, the South Koreans troops had broken and Chinese were pouring through a gap. They were moving southeast of us toward a place called Tokchong. If they got there, we would be encircled.

The ruckus to the near leftside, in the vicinity of the 23rd, was the frantic retreat of the 61st Artillery, which had been suddenly set upon by hundreds of shouting Chinese troops, who blew bugles as they raced through the freezing night. It was absolute panic.

The Chinese had gotten into position under cover of darkness and with great bravery. In 15-degree weather, they had taken off their pants and shoes and waded the freezing waters of the Chongchon, got dressed, then launched their attack.

Now, the firing that had been off to the left a half mile or so began to grow closer. Suddenly a mortar shell exploded near the headquarters tent. It set off a flurry of shouts and cries, and we scrambled to our shallow foxholes. The night had exploded with firing in all directions. More mortar shells detonated, bullets buzzed by.

Then a bugle sounded, followed by shouts; it seemed as though the earth disgorged a swarm of hunched figures, running toward us firing burp guns and shouting. Their uniforms had a silver hue to them in the light of the moon.

"Start shooting!" I hollered, an order that was not at all necessary. It was unlike anything I had seen on New Guinea or the Philippines. It was mass hysteria ... Chinese running everywhere, their movement lighted by the flares that hung in the night. Everyone was shouting, whistles and bugles blowing, grenades exploding, the gunsmoke hanging over the fields and the shallow defiles where men crawled, cried, and died. Madness. But in a way I relished it. It was living on the edge. This was the way it was for a soldier. I shouted and fired my weapon.

Some of the Chinese were jumping into foxholes and at times five or six of them would be crammed in. I crawled toward one group of them, tossed a grenade in, then stood and sprayed it with Tommy gun fire. Two of our guys ran up, checked it, then raised their right arms in a signal that the Chinese were dead. It was so cold that many of the weapons froze up. One man, I was told later, took care of that by urinating on the blasted thing; the heat warmed it sufficiently and he was able to continue the fight. I worked my way to where one of our Quad-50s was in action. This weapon is actually four 50-caliber Browning machine guns mounted on a wheeled vehicle. I climbed aboard and took over, spraying all four machine guns at a gulley from where the Chinese attack units were coming.

By the early morning hours of November 26, the Chinese

were thrown back across the river, but we were outside and awake for the remaining hours of darkness. With daylight, we found dead Chinese by the droves. At the river some of the poor souls lay in grotesque positions; some had been killed early in the battle, and had suffered the indignity of being cut down before they could get their pants on.

Those Chinese who survived had retreated to the high hills to the north. And from there, they could observe us and fire machine guns down our throats. And they did so.

In defense of the men of the 61st Artillery: they were not cowards. They had set their campsite near the river before the 23rd had arrived that afternoon, and the perimeter put up by A and B companies did not wrap around the artillery site. I don't guess it was anybody's fault, it just happened that way. No one knew the Chinese would attack. After all, we were the ones who were supposed to be attacking.

Personally, it angered me that we were hit by such surprise. We had known the Chinese were there . . . somewhere. But anyway, when daylight came the men of the 61st were sent back to occupy their camp and reclaim their weapons. I wanted to ask Col. Freeman if we still didn't need to worry about the Chinese on camels. But I never got the chance. And it wouldn't have been proper for me to bring it up.

KOREA BECAME A frozen hell and a frozen graveyard for many soldiers, American, South Koreans, and Chinese. The fighting was as bad as anything I'd seen in World War II. For the next two days and nights, the Chinese attacked almost constantly. They didn't come in "human wave" attacks as has been so often said, but they came in a well-disciplined assault plan. They'd pop mortar shells on us from the front, then send strong units of troops hitting us from the side and even from the rear.

They had very few radios, but relied on the bugle and the shepherd horn for signals to attack, hold, or withdraw. While we were bound to roadways — such as they were — the Chinese traveled along dry creek beds or ravines. In one case, an entire regiment of Chinese troops, about 2,000, ran along a dry creek bed for several miles, not turning one way or another, not uttering a word, and attacked the rear units of both the 2nd and 25th Divisions, creating such havoc that there was fear we were being encircled. Before long we would be.

On the night of November 27-28, I stayed in a foxhole and fired at Chinese Communist troops who just kept hitting at us. Sometimes they would attack with a bugle signal to warn us, other times they would suddenly rise up ten yards in front of us. I was nipped on the face just below the right eye by a piece of shrapnel from a grenade, but the cold seemed to close it off and there was little or no bleeding. It just stung. But it didn't hurt any more than the icy cold.

When daylight came the attackers withdrew, and I crawled back to find some hot coffee. There wasn't any. So I returned to the hole. Gibbons sprinted to my post and jumped in just as the machine guns on the heights opened up again, sending dirt and pepples flying as the bullets struck nearby.

"Cold enough?" he asked.

"Colder than a well-digger's ass," I replied.

"We're going to try to pull out of here," he said. "Word came down from division."

"Hell, I thought we were going to launch an all-out assault," I said sarcastically. "Hey, you remember me telling you about the Chinese on camels? I'll bet they believe it now back there."

Gibbons nodded. "I don't mind the camels, but I could

do without all these Chinese guys. There's too many of them, Lionel."

"When are we pulling out?" I asked.

Gibbons said we — meaning the 38th Regiment — were to make our way to the village of Kunu-ri, where all roads in the area met, then head south to Sunchon, about eight miles distant.

Before he left me, the lieutenant notified me that orders had come down on me. "You got your second award of the Combat Infantryman Badge," he said. Then, somewhat cynically, he added, "I know the folks back home are proud of you."

I laughed. "I doubt if my father is. This is my second war and he still thinks I'm a recruit."

11

Chinese Capture and Escape

THAT AFTERNOON SOME South Korean ammo bearers brought up some hot coffee. I was squatted down against a rock, took a big gulp of it, and closed my eyes. For a moment I saw Una and I saw my mother and remembered the aroma of her kitchen.

Then the machine guns opened up and I heard shouting and bugles. I opened my eyes and saw the world as it was at that moment: men running crazily; to my left was a long line of dead men laying on the ground, blankets over their faces.

I ran toward my post, but saw Chinese soldiers running by it. Nearby, an American soldier stopped running as through frozen in time, a spurt of blood coming from his face. Then he fell heavily. I fired several bursts from the Tommy gun then ran to the right toward a ravine, shouting at several men to follow. I didn't know where Gibbons was, I didn't see Leeming.

There were men running and tripping in front of me, some of them firing wildly into the air. I turned and saw Chinese behind me, firing. I shot back, then wheeled around and ran farther into the deep hollow, knocking over two American soldiers. One of them, his face contorted, was crying. I had a strange feeling that I wasn't getting out of this one.

There were Chinese troops everywhere — including a couple

on horseback. Beyond I saw a clump of American soldiers sit down suddenly. Just then a machine gun began firing from the far end of the hollow, a grazing fire that snapped right over our heads. I went down. There were Chinese in front of us and behind us and some in the deep ditch that ran at an oblique line to the high hills to the front.

"I'm hit," one man shouted.

Another cried, "My gun's jammed."

And another called, "Out of ammo. We gotta surrender."

Others took up the cry, "Gotta surrender."

Surrender, like hell, I thought. Desperately, I turned back to the southwest, toward the perimeter, but I saw nothing but a cluster of Chinese advancing, their weapons leveled at us. There was no shooting now, and the firing to my left suddenly seemed more distant. From the other direction another Chinese group came forward, keeping just to the south of the ditch to allow the machine gun to fire if need be. They were after prisoners. They had us.

I put the Tommy gun down easily with my right hand, raising the left one slightly, keeping my eyes on the Chinese. One of them toward the front, a thin guy with pock marks on his face, nodded at me as I put the weapon on the ground. Then he jerked his burp gun, indicating he wanted me to raise my hands and move back with the others. I did so. There wasn't much of a choice.

Now the Chinese ran up to us and began shouting orders, pushing and gesturing for us to move out to the north. On every American face I saw the same haunted expression: humiliation, fear, the dread of the unknown. A soldier captured is stripped of his pride, his spirit emasculated. A couple of the boys were critically wounded, and were left behind. They probably died. I had no idea who they were. I turned and looked back to what had been our defense line; in the distance I saw some of our guys running and shooting, pursued by Chinese who seemed to be just yards away. The running fight faded into the cold gray horizon.

"Son-of-a-bitch," I muttered.

A Chinese soldier gave me a push, saying, "G.I. son-bitch."

WE WERE HURRIED to a wide creek, a tributary to the Chongchon, and ordered to wade across. It was shallow, reaching just below my knees, but so cold that it took my breath away. There was a layer of ice, but it was too thin to hold. The temperature was around 15 degrees. I've never been so cold. One of the men, who was bleeding from a leg wound, collapsed. The Chinese ordered several men to carry him. We took turns. By late in the afternoon, the sounds of firing faded, and we were corralled in a ravine with about a hundred other Americans and some South Koreans.

It was a dismal and disheartening scene. There was a chance I would be killed or spend the rest of my life in a POW camp somewhere in Manchuria or China. As we sat there, several Chinese soldiers kept watch. Meanwhile some built a fire and others brought up a pot and began cooking rice. Later, they allowed us to build fires. I still had some crackers in my pocket plus some packets of instant coffee. I melted snow in my canteen cup, then poured the mix into it. Army instant coffee is usually terrible, but that was the best cup I'd tasted. It warmed my insides.

As we sat in the snow and cold wind, I took stock of what had happened. The first thing was to stay as warm as possible. Most of us had earlier discarded our helmets in favor of the fur pile caps, which kept your head warm. You could untie the flaps and bring them down over your ears. I tied mine down around my ears and pulled a third flap across my face. Then I closed my eyes, resting. But my mind was racing. I had to get out of here. The best chance to get away is early in a capture. We were still within a day's march of American troops and we were not in a wired compound.

Then, from a small hill above us, I heard a voice calling us to attention. A Chinese officer spoke in pretty good English, telling us that we were prisoners and would be treated fairly.

"If you try to run, you will be shot," he warned. "There is nowhere for you Joes to go. We control the land. We will kill you or you will die in the snow. You rest. We march tonight."

Then he left. We were in an open area and the wind was brutal.

March tonight, hell, I thought. They didn't want our air guys to see us. They would hide us during the day, and make us march northward during the night. As we huddled in the ravine tryng to keep warm, we were ordered to remain still. If we had to urinate we had to stand where we were and do it. We were not allowed to move away from the others. It was an agonizing time for the wounded. When evening came, I finished off my crackers, made the last of my coffee before the fire was put out, and sat studying the situation.

We sat close together to help keep warm. So I said to those in earshot: "This thing is not going to get any better for us. I'm taking off when I see a chance to make a break for it."

"When you going?" one of them asked. All were looking at me, their faces pulled back in frozen snarls, their eyes bright with anger and fear.

"When I see a chance," I said. "It's going to be quick. When I go, I'm going. If you want to go you'll be on your own. I won't be able to wait on you."

None of us had any hope that we would be rescued. The Chinese controlled the battlefield. To the south, the night sky pulsated with artillery bursts and flares. I figured we must not be more than a dozen miles from where we had been captured.

Then, the Chinese ordered us to form up and move out. Guards with burp guns were posted along the edge of the column at intervals of about ten yards. The trail was along a ridge line. It was rough, full of rocks and depressions, and some of the men fell several times. The Chinese were in such a hurry to get moving that they did not take extra precautions with us, such as tying us together. I figured they would do that later.

I didn't know the men who were with me and didn't know if they could be counted on in an escape. But I whispered to those nearest me that I was going to go for it shortly. "Get ready."

If we didn't go then, we might never get a chance. They passed the word silently.

Now we were along a flat ridge where the ground seemed fairly level. To the east, in the darkness I could make out the outline of another shoulder rising above the hill. I watched the guard on my side of the column pause and turn to view the others coming up behind me. I shot a glance behind me; he was still looking to the rear.

Impulsively, I slapped the arm of the man to my left then sprang to the right, toward the east, and ran through the night, across the ridge, my body bent forward, my shoulders hunched, awaiting the burst of automatic weapons fire that would rip into my back. I heard others running behind me, but I didn't know if they were GIs or Chinese. I didn't stop to look; I couldn't look back. I kept running due east up the hill. The sound of my boots crunching in the snow was deafening. I knew the guards heard it.

I cringed, waiting for the bullets to come. But nothing happened. There was only the sound of my feet and my breathing and the thumping in my chest. Now, I was in a clump of small scrubby trees; branches slapped my face and almost tore the pile cap off my head.

"Oh, Jesus Christ help us," I said to myself.

Where were the shouts and where were the shots and the flying bullets? Nothing happened.

"They'll get you in the back, Pinn," I said. "Oh, Jesus Christ, help us."

I kept running, waiting for the bullets. But none came. I heard nothing. There was only my chest pounding, and I ran harder than I ever ran before.

Then faintly I heard a whistle blast, followed instantly by shouts. Then came the shots. Brrrpp. Brrrppp. Now more whistles blew. I didn't look back. Somebody cried out, "I'm hit. Wait, wait. Bastards!"

We kept running. I had no idea how many were with me. Again came the sound of burp guns stuttering in the cold air, the echoes bouncing through the hills. The sound seemed to come from all around.

The frigid air was freezing my lungs, but I kept up the pace. Now the sounds of gunfire ceased. We slowed to a trot and kept it up for nearly an hour. The men behind me were begging to halt and rest. Finally I turned, and waited. There were six men with me. One was bleeding from a shoulder wound. Another sank to the ground, clutching his lower legs.

A few flakes of snow fell; the wind was unforgiving. Behind us, to the west, we heard bugles and whistles blowing. The hunt was on.

"We gotta keep moving," I said. "And don't talk."

My best guess was that we had covered about four miles since leaving the group, moving east into the hills. If the ground had been level, we'd have covered seven or eight miles. I was concerned about the snow. We had to move on.

"Come on, men, let's move," I said. "If the snow gets heavy we'll be easy to track. And it will be hard to move."

"Where we going?" one asked. "How far are we from our lines?"

"Who knows," I said. "We were retreating."

Then I turned north along the ridgeline. "Let's go."

"Hey, south is this way," one of them said.

"I know," I said. "That's why we're going this way."

The men stared at me.

"Look, they expect us to go south," I said. "That's where they'll look. We go north, then cut back later, and move south on the other side of this ridge. It'll be longer, but we'll stand a better chance."

Two of the six agreed, the others muttered obscenities and turned south. I moved out at a trot, followed by the two. I never asked them their names. I wasn't interested in knowing.

WE MOVED NORTH for two hours, then found a cave where we rested. We were going to spend the day there resting, but something told me there would be Chinese and North Koreans who would be searching the caves. The snow came down steadily. While it was still light, we hurried out and crossed the ridge, then headed south. We ate snow, found an abandoned farm house with some carrots in a storage shed, slept for another hour, then ran until we found an overhanging rock. We crawled under it and slept. I thought we would freeze. I dreamed of cornbread and beef stew and hot coffee.

On the third day, we stumbled into a valley and heard voices. I dove into a ditch and the others followed. We waited in the icy ditch until we heard the group approaching, talking in low voices. It had to be Chinese, I thought. Our luck was running out. I heard and felt the group pass by and then I eased up to take a look. To my relief, they weren't Chinese. They were Republic of Korea troops, South Koreans.

"They're ROKs," I said aloud, standing and waving. "They're ROKs."

At first the South Koreans put their weapons on us, but a lieutenant muttered an order and they lowered them. Several of them spoke English and told us they had been cut off when the Chinese invaded. These troops had been almost to the Yalu River. Now, they were trying to get back to their lines, fearful that the Chinese would get them.

Most of the South Koreans were without weapons, having thrown them down in their haste to flee. But they had some food, which they shared with us. It took us another two days to get back to our lines, which were still fluid and in retreat. The other two Americans with me went their own way as we ran into our troops. I figured we had walked fifty miles.

When I finally reached the 38th Regiment, the unit was almost back in South Korea; the camp was in disarray.

"Where the hell have you been?" a captain asked when I reported to the headquarters tent. "You look like hell."

"Where have I been?" I replied. "Hell's fire, I've been captured. I was a prisoner. That's where I've been. I almost got my ass shot off escaping. If I look bad, I could care less, sir. I'm just glad to be living."

The captain reported my return to a major who glared at me and asked, "Where the hell you been?"

"Captured, sir," I said sarcastically. "Maybe I should have stayed there."

Then I walked away without saluting the SOB. The 38th, as well as the entire 2nd Infantry Divison, had been butchered as it withdrew from Kuni-ri to Sunchon. Chinese troops massed on the hillsides and poured deadly fire onto the narrow road that was the escape route. Most of the boys in my platoon had been casualties.

Ed Leeming was gone. He had been wounded during the retreat and had been airlifted out, I was told. I didn't know how bad he might have been hit. I didn't know where Coyle was. Lt. Gibbons had been badly wounded when a jeep he was riding in had been hit by Chinese mortar fire or a grenade. I didn't know which.

In all the confusion I went to find something to eat, and some hot coffee. The war would have to wait. A cook got me a piece of bread, some hash, and a big canteen cup full of coffee. Even as I sat on the ground eating, the unit was packing up, preparing for another retreat. In all, it would be a retreat of over 150 miles, the longest in U.S. history. We had gotten the hell beat out of us again.

To the east, about eighty miles or so, the 1st Marine Division fought its way out to the sea. The Army's 7th Infantry Division was bloodied like we had been. I heard stories of another "Custer's Last Stand" where a column of 2,500 men of the 7th Division had been ambushed; only 1,050 survived.

I packed my few belongings, got into a truck, and fell asleep. When I awoke that night, we were somewhere around Seoul, the South Korean capital.

THE ARMY SENT me off the line and had me report to a field

hospital which looked like it just been set up in haste. A doctor, a captain who had probably been drafted, gave me a brief check-up.

Then another captain, who was a psychologist or psychiatrist, came in and asked me what was making me so angry.

"I guess just being here, sir," I said. "I've been wounded, my teeth knocked out, colder than hell, then I get captured and escape and everybody is pissed off at me for showing back up. How do you expect me to feel?"

"Did somebody say they didn't believe you had been captured?" he asked.

I shrugged. "Sir, they didn't have to. All of them kept asking me where I'd been. I guess I should have had the Chinese send me a note home. I guess I'm angry because we all thought we had the thing won, then this happens."

"You mean the Chinese coming in?"

"Yes, sir. We knew they were coming. I seen them on camels. But nobody listened. The brass knew they were coming in."

They sent me to a rest area around Pusan for a few days. I got to shower and put on clean clothes, fresh green from the supply dump. Made me look like a recruit. Some of the men at the rest area told me where there were Korean prostitutes, but I passed. I never messed with any of the native women.

THERE WAS ALMOST a complete change in the 38th, as dozens of strangers came in as replacements. I got back from the rest area in time to fight another big battle with the Chinese at Hoenchon. It was almost as bad as the Chongchon. I never got over being angry about everything. I wanted to be the best soldier I could be, but somehow, some of the leadership was lacking. There were good officers, certainly, but from time to time there was a man who would show up who didn't need to be in charge of anybody.

One day in March 1951 we were attacking a hill and were waiting for the Air Force to soften up the place. Jets swooped down and dropped napalm. Then we moved up. We heard some of the Chinese guys moaning and trying to speak as they died from the burns. Most had been killed almost instantly. Suddenly this Chinese soldier staggered out. He was covered with napalm burns. He had his hands raised. He looked horrible.

Some of the men ran to him and a medic came up. The Chinese guy, he was just a kid, sat down and began talking to us in a rapid-fire delivery. One of our men gave him a piece of bread. He took a bite of it. Then he shook his head. He said something else, then sat on the ground holding the bread.

I turned and saw a chunky captain standing there, gazing down on the Chinese guy. Then he told me to have the kid shot.

"Hell, Captain, we just can't kill him," I said.

"He's asking us to do it," the captain said. "You do it, Sarge. Put the poor bastard away."

I looked at the Chinese kid then back at the captain. "I'm not shooting him," I said. "If you want him dead, you do it. Then I guess you can shoot me, too."

The captain drew his .45 out of the holster and took quick aim, and fired. The kid lurched sideways. But he kept twitching and jumping.

"God damn it, Captain, he's still not dead," I said. "He's still suffering, you bastard."

The captain walked away and the kid's body jumped around for several seconds, then he went quiet. I wanted to take my Tommy gun and shoot the captain. But I didn't.

12

Leaving Korea

IN THE SUNLIGHT of an April afternoon the high hills showed splashes of green here and there as the last patches of snow melted away. The slushy remains sent little rivulets of muddy water sluicing down the slopes. It was chilly, but there was warmth in the sun. We were in the rear area for a break; I had found the mess tent where there was hot coffee and some bread and Army stew. I was sitting on the hood of a jeep when I noticed a figure from a distance walking toward me.

There were dozens of men in the area, but this one stood out, something about the way he walked. I stopped eating and watched him approach, his M-1 rifle slung across his shoulder.

"My God," I said, almost dropping my food. "It's Leeming."

He was walking toward me, a big grin spreading across his face. "Hey, you crazy Indian," he called.

"You made it," I said, standing up. "I thought maybe the Chinks got you back at Kunu-ri."

"They shot me but they couldn't keep me down," he quipped, a bit of John Wayne swagger in his voice.

We gave each other a hug. Then he stepped back. "Did you get hit? Never knew what happened. I thought maybe you were dead."

"Naw. They caught me for a few days, but I got away."

He laughed. "I didn't think they could get you."

Ed had been seriously wounded during the retreat on November 30, and had been sent to a military hospital in Japan. Now he was back, assigned to another unit of the 2nd Division. We visited for a little while, then he had to go on. He was my best friend in Korea. When he walked away, I didn't know if I would ever see him again.

The war had been fast-paced during the first year or so, with a lot of movement up and down the Korean Peninsula. But by the late summer of 1951 it had settled into the bloody business of both sides dug in near the 38th Parallel, the boundary between North Korea and South Korea. It became a bloody contest over one hill or another, mostly bald, rugged rises that had little or no tactical value. We would attack a hill, lose a number of men, finally take it, then find ourselves facing another hill after that.

My weapon of preference was always the Thompson submachine gun, which was my companion in the jungles of New Guinea and the Philippines. It was also a life-saver in Korea. Most of the men in both wars used the Garand M-1, which was a marvelous rifle with great power and accuracy. The problem with it was that it only held eight bullets. And the greater problem, as a lot of guys discovered in Korea, was that when that eighth bullet was fired, the clip ejected from the top of the weapon with a loud PING! sound. I saw this downfall on a cold January day in 1951 while on a patrol. The Chinese and the revamped North Korean Army were still pushing at us, but we had stabilized.

Our patrol came under fire from the high ground. Two of the men got behind a rocky outcrop on the lower slope. They began returning fire, as did the rest of us. I was down the way from them, in a broad, but shallow ditch that smelled of runoff from a rice paddy. The Chinese were firing, tossing grenades, and trying to outflank us. But they were also threatening a full frontal assault, and I was busy firing to my front. Then, to the left, I saw some Chinese troops move closer to the position where those two guys were. As I watched, I heard a ping-ping sound. Both men had fired their last round at the same time. Within a second the Chinese were on their feet racing forward.

Before the guys could get reloaded, the Chinese had tossed a grenade and then moved all the way in, firing their burp guns. I fired a long burst from my Tommy gun and that bought some time, but one of the guys was hit by the burp gun. If they had had more firepower, they would have had a better chance to save themselves and hold their ground.

In September 1951 my tour of duty was over and I left the place, sailed to Japan and went through the processing centers, which included the refitting of uniforms plus the numerous medical check-ups. There were long lines of naked men who stood with unabashed pride as they waited for the doctor. They had survived.

From the infantryman's point of view, the American troops in Korea had undergone a birth of fire, changing from green, lackluster rookies to one of the best field armies in history. Many of them were draftees who had been thrown into the pot. They did well against a determined enemy. The Chinese fought hard, fought bravely; so did most of the Americans.

When I left Japan, I waved a quiet farewell as the boat eased away. It was not only good-bye to Japan, but to that part of the world. I felt it was not likely I would ever return that way. This had been my second war; the odds were it would be the last. And if there was to be another, it would likely be against the Russians. Before leaving Japan, I had thought about finding the family of the Japanese soldier I had killed on New Guinea. I still had his personal belongings. I somehow wanted to do that. But the Army officially advised me it would not be a good idea.

We arrived in California about twenty days later. There were some families waiting for their sons and husbands, but not much of a welcome generally. It wasn't like World War II in that respect. I was given back pay, then caught a train headed east. My orders were to report in thirty days to Fort Benning, Georgia. On the train ride I couldn't help but gawk out the windows as the American countryside flashed by. This is what we had fought for, wasn't it? I wanted to get a horse and ride across the desert and up to the mountaintops. I was alive and basically in good shape. There was an exuberant spirit inside me that wanted to soar and touch every ounce of life.

I spent most of the time with Una and later went to Massachusetts to see my mother. Dad was overseas again. Then I reported to Fort Benning, where I was assigned to an infantry training unit. My job once again was to teach recruits. But I wanted something more. I wanted to dive out of a plane, and sent in a request for airborne training. It was turned down. My arms just were not up to par. I vowed to change that. When I got a chance, I would go to the gym to lift weights and do pull-ups. Then I would jog around the post, mile after mile.

The company commander, a captain, grew tired of me asking to go for airborne training. In the fall of 1952 I went out for the post football team and made it as an end. I was twenty-nine years old. Most of the guys were officers just out of college where they had played. I liked the hard hitting. The training was tough, but not any more rugged that I had been through. Besides, when you play football, you know the idea is only to tackle somebody, not kill them, or be killed yourself. It was fun and good for my physical conditioning. I was pretty fast and liked making hard, clean tackles. But I mostly enjoyed the thrill of chasing down a long pass and catching it.

By early 1953 the Army transferred me to the 30th Regimental Combat team and we were sent on an assignment that was rated Secret. We joined several thousand other troops in the Nevada desert to take part in Operation Desert Rock — an operation in an area where an atomic bomb was to be detonated. We were to be placed in a trench about two miles from the site of the blast, then later were to move forward. The idea was to see how well soldiers could survive at such close range to a nuclear explosion, then be monitored for the amount of radiation that might be absorbed.

We were sort of used as guinea pigs. There were actually four blasts that I experienced. I always kept my head down and my eyes closed. But some of the guys couldn't resist taking a look; some of them paid for it, suffering eye damage. I wasn't aware at the time of any health problems, but the effects of radiation are sometimes long-term. Only later in life would I feel the full impact of having been there.

AFTER THE ATOMIC tests I finally agreed with the Army that there might be more to life than the infantry. I was a sergeant first-class and there were many easier jobs around. One of them was being a mess sergeant, the guy in charge of the food service. I decided to go after it, and was sent to Fort Belvoir, Virginia.

But once an infantry sergeant, always an infantry sergeant. The Army assigned me to head a hospital mess hall. It was hard work from a mental standpoint, keeping up with the food orders and other paperwork. It wasn't long before it annoyed me.

But what really rankled me was the attitude of the soldiers

in the hospital. They thought they could just eat what they wanted, and if they didn't like it they'd send it back and whine for something else.

One day I went into the wards and this guy who had a dislocated knee or something was lying there with his hands behind his head, taking life easy. He hadn't touched his lunch.

"Why didn't you eat?" I asked him. "Food not like Mom's?"

"I guess I just wasn't too hungry," he said. "I'll ask the nurse to get me something a little later."

"Oh, I see," I said, feigning civility. "Just ring for service, huh?"

He looked up at me and studied my ribbons for a moment. Then he said, "Look, Sarge, I didn't ask to be here."

"Well, you are here and you're going to damn well eat what we've got," I said. "I'll have the cooks put up your tray with your name on it. When it's time for the evening meal, I'll send it back to you. And I'll keep doing that until you eat it."

I did other men the same way. It wasn't that I was trying to be mean. But I felt a soldier has to learn to take what he gets. A lot of good men died in Korea who would have considered this food a feast. But lecturing goldbricks wasn't much of a challenge, and I again put in for airborne training — and again I failed the physical training test.

It angered me that the Army would not make some allowance for my combat experience. While I was awaiting my chance to do the pull-ups, the kid behind me said, "Sarge, you think it's scary jumping out of a plane?"

I turned around. "Scary? Hell, I've been shot at in two wars and almost got killed four or five times. Jumping out of a plane is going to be a friggin' breeze, boy, a friggin' breeze."

My failure to get into the paratrooper training began to rile me a lot; I was getting restless. Being a mess sergeant wasn't what I wanted out of life. I started spending nights in Washington, hanging out in some bars on 16th Street, N.W., sometimes getting crocked on good bourbon.

One evening I started talking to a civilian, a husky, dark-haired man with a ready smile. He was a deep bronze, obviously an American Indian. I mentioned that I was in the Army (at the time I was in civilian clothing).

He chuckled. "Dogface, huh?"

"Yeah, I guess so," I said. "What about you?"

"From the Halls of Montezuma," he said, flashing a friendly but challenging smile.

"Marines," I said. "Good outfit." Then I asked, "You have to go overseas?"

He nodded, took another drink, then grinned at me. "Remember the flag on Iwo Jima?"

I shrugged. "Well, hell yeah, I remember seeing the picture."

"I was one of 'em," he said.

I sat back and took a better look at him. "The hell you say."

He responded by lifting his glass in a high salute. And then he took another drink.

"What's your name?"

"Ira Hayes," he said. "I'm the Indian." And in the same breath he called to the bartender, "More firewater."

I raised my hand. "The hell with one more drink, bring us two more each," I said, a bit too loudly. "You hear who this guy is? He was one of them that put the flag up on the hill on Iwo Jima. Hell, you oughta give us a free bottle."

The bartender was not impressed. He poured us a drink and waited for us to pay.

I slapped Hayes on the shoulder. "My mom is Micmac and my dad is an Osage."

He nodded in quiet appreciation. But, as luck would have it, at that precise moment a group of four or five young Marines walked in, all spit and polish in their green uniforms. Hayes, who had been in a friendly mood, turned and glared at them. Then he called them something like "you mess of skinny-ass jarheads" and some other choice remarks. Next thing I know the young Marines were on us and we were getting pushed and knocked out the front door.

As I picked myself up off the sidewalk, Hayes was laughing at me. I didn't think anything was funny. "Hey, you landed a couple of good ones," he said. "You didn't do bad."

"Thanks," I said. "Next time you plan to start a war how about letting me in on it. You know, if those guys knew who you were they wouldn't have hit you."

Hayes wiped his mouth and chuckled. "Yeah, they threw some good ones, too."

Ira Hayes and I became drinking pals for a time, hob-nobbing around some of the Washington bars and even some parties in the suburbs. He lived on a reservation in Arizona, and had come to the Capital to be a part of the ceremony unveiling the monument to the flag-raising on Iwo Jima. One night we walked along Pennsylvania Avenue, arms around each other, singing "Bye, Bye, Blackbird." After several minutes, Ira just stopped singing, stood there in the chill night air, then turned and punched me in the jaw. It knocked me to the sidewalk. I got up slowly, then asked, "Why'd you do that?" He laughed. "Because you were the closest guy, Chooch."

I nodded. "I see." Then I hit him with a right cross that sent him sprawling on his back.

He staggered to his feet and by the light of a street lamp I could see a grin crinkle across his face. "Why'd you do that?"

"I don't know, Ira," I said.

The drinking was really getting to be a serious problem. I was getting in late and sometimes had trouble getting ready for duty in the mornings. But since I was in charge of a mess hall it wasn't much of a problem, as I rarely had to see anyone who was a superior. But in the Army there's always someone who is in charge and in my case it was a colonel who was a stickler for military discipline. So one morning I was awakened by a corporal who informed me that the colonel wanted to see me on the double.

"God Almighty," I muttered. "What time is it?"

"Eight-thirty, sergeant," the corporal replied, then backed away.

I was to have been on duty by 8 a.m. There was hardly time to take a shower. I must have smelled like a brewery.

"I'm going to have to clean up," I said.

"He said right away, sergeant," the soldier said, looking apologetic as he reached for the door to leave.

I nodded and hurried into a class A uniform. There wasn't time to shave or anything. I could have brushed my teeth, but when your system is full of whisky the odor seeps out. Only one thing hides it.

I threw on my uniform and headed for the colonel's office, but on the way there I stopped by the mess hall, went into the storage area, and got an onion. A big raw one. Then I took a big bite of it, and chewed it quickly.

Then I strode boldly into the colonel's office. The clerk,

seated behind a small desk near the door, rose quickly to block me, but I brushed by him.

Entering the room, I stopped, flipped a salute and barked, "Morning, Colonel!"

He glanced up. "Morning, Pinn, I wanted—Good God, what in hell is that smell?"

"Sir?" I feigned puzzlement.

"That smell, Pinn. My God, what've you been eating this time of morning?"

"Oh, that." I chuckled. "It's onions, sir."

"I know it's onions, sergeant. I wasn't born yesterday."

"Well, sir, I have a bad cold, and onions eaten raw are a remedy," I said. "That's been a tradition among my Indian ancestors and has been passed on to us."

He waved at me in disgust, and then talked to me about my reports from the mess hall. Then, he excused me.

"Next time you get a cold, go see one of our doctors," he said.

"Yes, sir."

As I was leaving I saw him glance up with a quizzical look. "I never knew Indians were fond of onions."

I left without answering.

Ira Hayes dropped out of sight and I spent less time in Washington. Ira drank too much, way too much. But he was a warrior. He was like my Dad. Dad came to Washington and I met him one evening for dinner. Our family life had changed a lot in two wars. He and Mom had separated. Even though he was in his middle fifties, Dad was a fine specimen of a man. We talked little. Then, he glanced at my chest, with the ribbons topped by the blue Combat Infantryman Badge.

"Well, son," he said, finally, "I guess without me really knowing it you just sort of grew up. For a time I didn't know how you would turn out, but I think you've done OK."

"OK?" I smiled. "Dad, I survived two wars." My father's eyes grew hard and bright and looked right through me. He leaned forward.

"No, you just didn't survive, you fought in two wars," he said. "There's a difference. You did good." I shrugged and nodded. "Come on," he said, "let's go to the bar. I'll buy you a beer."

We drank a couple of bottles of imported brew, then he told me he was going back overseas to the Middle East. His unit was involved in a project in the Persian Gulf.

I told him I wanted to be a paratrooper. "Then do it," he said. "You can do what you want." Then, it was time to depart. We didn't know when we might see each other again.

As he got up to leave, I rose with him and extended a hand. He took it with both of his and squeezed hard.

"I love you, son," he said.

I nodded. "Thanks, Dad. I love you. And you think I've turned out OK, huh?"

He nodded, then produced a big Mexican cigar out of his vest pocket, unwrapped it and gave it to me. I grinned at him, then put the cigar in my mouth, and fumbled for a light.

"Hold it," he said. "Allow me."

He borrowed a candle from a nearby table and held it up. I puffed a cloud of smoke. Then he slapped me on the shoulder and walked out, his back straight, his head erect, putting his cap on as he strode away, looking neither to the right nor to the left.

I sat at the bar puffing on the cigar.

Dad went back to the Middle East. About a year later I was notified that he had contacted some type of virus caused by a desert mite. He had been hospitalized. The next day, December

20, 1954, another telegram came saying that Dad had died.

They buried him at Arlington. It had been one of Dad's wishes that he be buried there, although he had not expected it to be so soon. When the bugler blew Taps, I saluted. But I wept, too.

A few months later I was back in Washington and went to visit Dad's grave. As I looked about at some of the other markers, I noticed one not far away for my old drinking buddy, Ira Hayes. He had died January 15, 1955, less than a month after Dad. In fact, Ira and Dad are pretty close together. On the register, Master Sergeant Carl Pinn is in Section 34, grave No. 504-A. Ira Hayes, former Marine, is in Section 34, grave No. 479-N. In death, they are close enough to be buddies. They would have made a tough team. And nearby is the grave of Gen. "Black Jack" Pershing.

Lionel Pinn's father, M/Sgt. Carl Pinn, above left and right, was a proud member of the Osage tribe and a career soldier. He set high standards for his son.

Left, Lionel's mother, Lucy Charles Pinn, was a Micmac Indian. Here she is holding young Lionel Pinn, in a photo taken around 1924.

After entering the Army in 1940, a boyish Lionel, right, shown on a visit home with younger brother, Carl Pinn, Jr.

Lionel, right, with his father, Carl, and younger brother, Carl, Jr., a sailor, in a post-WWII photo.

Left, Pinn with a captured Japanese flag, during World War II.

Below, at Fort Lewis, Washington, Pinn (right) talks with men of his platoon. This was shortly before sailing for Korea in 1950.

A photo from a newsmagazine covering the Korean War caught the cigar-chomping Pinn, then a sergeant with the 2nd Infantry Division, questioning young North Korean prisoners.

After his tour in Korea, Pinn, shown here at top right, was given winter training. "It was the last thing I needed after the winter in Korea," he quipped.

Left, in dress uniform after the Korean War.

Below: A slimmed-down Pinn in a photo taken in the late 1950s, just before becoming a Green Beret.

Another war, another cigar: Pinn talks with Lao militia trainees in 1962.

In Laos, Pinn, right, with Lt. Robert G. Lunday, left, and Sgt. Lawrence P. Schell.

Above: This Polaroid shot was taken by Pinn's captors when he was a river doctor captured by Pathet Lao in July 1962. He later managed to get away. Below: In Vietnam with 4th Infantry in 1966: Standing guard while commanders map out a battle plan.

Above, Pinn in Vietnam in 1967.

Right, a vintage Pinn, with cigar in hand, taken near his retirement in 1970.

PART THREE

LAOS & VIETNAM

13

Fort Benning

I WENT TO Fort Benning, Georgia, in 1955 and was made the first sergeant in an infantry training company. I had fanagled the assignment, because Benning is where they train you to be a paratrooper. Since I was the first sergeant, I kept putting myself on orders for jump school. I would fail the physical and wash out, but then I'd turn right around and cut orders sending me back the next cycle.

Arthur "Bull" Simon, the legendary officer who was in charge of the Ranger school at the fort, saw me one day. Bristling with humor, he said, "Pinn, you are the most persistent SOB I've ever seen."

"Thank you, sir," I said, saluting with a little extra zip in it. Finally in 1955 I passed the paratrooper physical and went on to make my first jump, the first of many. I actually breezed through it.

On landing after that first one, I gave a whoop and asked those nearby, "What's the big deal?"

I later volunteered for Special Forces training. While it was the toughest training I'd ever undergone, it wasn't beyond the reach of a thirty-three-year-old. I hated being called "the old man." I not only had to keep up with younger guys, I had to outdo them. At last, I had found a home in the Army. An infantryman at heart,

I still wanted something more out of the military life.

This was it. Special Forces was a big jump up from even the Alamo Scout training. I was running from five to fifteen miles a day.

In the late 1950s I was sent to Germany and did some training exercises there. We worked along the borders of Hungary, Czechoslovakia, and East Germany.

In 1960 I came home and voted for John Kennedy of Massachusetts, the first Catholic with a real chance to win. When he did, one of the first things he did was authorize the Special Forces to wear the green berets as part of our uniform. Before long, we were more often called Green Berets, although some of the older men preferred SF. While Cuba took a lot of attention, the real hot spot was Southeast Asia, especially Laos. The powers-that-be in Washington were convinced that if Laos fell the dominoes would roll and everything else would fall, and America would lose prestige.

Like Vietnam and Cambodia, Laos was in the middle of a struggle between Communist rebels and the American-backed government. That was the simple way to look at it. Actually, it was such a complex struggle that I don't believe we ever really understood any of it. In Laos, the people in the rural areas were caught in the middle, leaning toward whichever side was winning.

There had been American advisors in all three countries for years, and it was clear that one day some of us were going to be headed that way, in all probability, Laos.

14

'Listen to the Rice Grow'

THE ORDERS WERE dated 26 January 1962 from the Secretary of the Army to the commanding officer of the 7th Special Forces Group Fort Bragg, North Carolina.

We were to proceed on or about 9 February for Bangkok, Thailand and from there to Laos. There were 36 in our group, although once there we were to break into teams of six or eight.

The commander already in Laos was my old friend, Lt. Col. Arthur "Bull" Simon.

My team, known as FTT-1A -39, was commanded by Lt. Robert G. Lunday. Others in the group included M/Sgt. Frank Nolen Jr., S/Sgt. Lawrence P. Schell, Sgt. James A. Price and SFC Frank Taylor. Taylor and I joked about this kind of war, how different it would be from World War II and Korea, when we went on boats for days, getting seasick and lugging around steel helmets and equipment. How different it was to get aboard a big airplane and fly to the place in a matter of hours, carrying leather luggage and wearing civilian clothes.

The military flew us to Thailand, and from there we were put aboard the so-called "Air America" craft, a plane operated by the CIA. It took us to Luang Prabang, the old capital of Laos, and also the name of the province. Our ultimate destination would be the province of Nam Tha, which lay on the northwestern part of the country. From there we would range over the outlands.

From the air it was beautiful country, miles of unbroken tropical forests and spectacular high hills engulfed in wispy clouds; there was only an occasional patchwork of rice paddies and small clusters of houses where the villages slumbered in the great quilt of green. The craft banked and circled, then squared off in a shallow approach dive. The plane rolled to a halt.

A local police officer pointed us to where several buses were parked, buses that were already crowded with people and some animals in cages. Our team boarded one of them, which we were told would take us to Nam Tha.

Luang Prabang was a hive of people moving up and down narrow streets, a few cars grinding along the dirt street, people shouting, carts blocking traffic, chickens and geese squawking at sidewalk markets, and lovely women dressed in bright garb.

The bus headed out of town and soon we were on a narrow dirt road. I sat beside a wiry old man with a trace of a white goatee that flowed from his chin like a white waterfall. He looked like an Oriental prophet. He nodded solemnly when I sat down, but said nothing.

The man's air of wisdom brought to mind the old adage we heard about Laos that went:

"The Vietnamese plant rice; the Cambodians harvest it; the Laotians listen to it grow."

As the bus bounced along, I thought about the mission. We were part of what was called the White Star Mobile Training Team. Ostensibly, we were just plain Americans who had come over to help the people of Laos—help them with things like building schools and providing flood protection, even assist in medical and dental care. I don't know anyone naive enough to have believed that. Of course, the main thing was to help train the local militias to fight the Reds.

At that point we were without weapons. My Tommy gun and the other weapons had been shipped separately and were to be awaiting us when we arrived at our destination, Muong-Met.

After more than two hours on the bus, the driver pulled over and stopped, then turned and gestured to us. "All Americans out here," he said. "All Americans out here."

He smiled warmly and held the door open. I bowed to the old chap who had sat silently beside me. I wondered if he understood me, and whether he was with us or the Communist rebels, known as the Pathet Lao.

As though reading my thoughts, he said, "All Americans out here."

He bowed to me, and I bowed back.

We debarked in an isolated area where a narrow trail intersected the dirt road. We saw a young fellow with a mule and a rickety cart, presumably our escort to our village.

"Follow me, please," he said, with a slight bow.

We piled our gear onto the cart, what we could get on it, tied some more to the poor old mule, and toted the rest ourselves.

Lt. Lunday asked the guide, "We walk?"

The young man nodded. "Walk."

We had hoped for a truck or some jeeps. "How far?" I asked.

The young man smiled. "Not far."

It turned out "not far" was a two-day walk. It meant an overnight camp along the dirt road, surrounded by the unnerving little sounds that come from a tropical night. We had no weapons but I had made some hasty preparations. Grandfather Joe Charles had long ago taught me how to make a crude spear by sharpening a slender rock and tying it firmly to the end of a long, sturdy branch. I stood guard the first watch. Luckily, I didn't have to thrust at anybody or anything. We finally arrived in a village in Nam Tha and I was greeted by a tall, lean man named Jimmy Dean, a sergeant. Jimmy had been in Laos since September 1961. His tour and that of his fellow team members would soon be ended.

15

Prelude to Vietnam

THE SUN CAME up hot and muggy over the distant tree line bringing a steam-like vapor rising from the nearby rice paddies. Birds chattered and whistled; the village was rousing, the aroma of tea and rice cakes hanging heavily in the air.

We were lodged in a frame house that looked like it belonged on the lower side of the Bowery, a house that was not bad, only in need of a little fixing up. It had been the home of a French missionary; there was even a piano in the parlor. The rafter beams were exposed and provided not only support for the roof, but also served as a bridge for dozens of rats who nightly raced across them. They made good targets for those of us who perfected the use of the cross bow.

A Laotian woman, who was in her fifties, prepared breakfast and made coffee. After eating I went out to look over my troops.

There were about twenty or thirty of them. They ranged in age from young to middle-aged guys with poor vision and missing teeth. We were to train them to be government soldiers, men who would fight to support Defense Minister Phoumi in the battle against the Pathet Lao.

The enemy was supported by the communist North Vietnamese government in Hanoi as well as their communist allies in South Vietnam, called the Viet Cong.

From our briefings, it seemed the war—actually a bunch of isolated skirmishes—was not going well for the Phoumi government. Dean told us there had been a lull in recent days, but attacks could come at any time, and any village could be a target.

My first look at the government militia we were to train was an impression that would stick with me forever. They were a sorry-looking group, which is the best I can say. They were dressed in shabby clothing and seemed disinterested in the crisis that their country faced.

"You can tell they were trained by the French," I muttered. "I hope to hell I never have to go into combat with these jokers."

Another concern I had was that these men got to bring their wives with them. I thought it might be a problem at first, but later believed the women probably would have made better soldiers than the men. They trailed along, carried weapons and ammo and food, cooked, and in general were more likely to follow orders than the men.

For some reason, I don't why, I trusted most of the women in the village, but few of the men. Most of the women were intelligent, quite beautiful, and surprisingly strong. Most of them had husbands in the units. The men, as far as I could tell, were not trustworthy, and a lot of them, I would learn soon enough, were double agents. And they didn't make good soldiers. We tried like hell to bond them into a fighting unit, but the Pathet Lao would outclass them all the time.

ONE DAY IN early March we were alerted that a group of Pathet Lao, number unknown, was in the jungle moving toward us. Lunday told us to take out patrols and beat the guerrillas at their own game. The aim was to get into position and maybe spring a trap or, at the very least, catch them off guard and turn them around before the village could be attacked.

It was a good game plan. But naturally, as we would find out, a good game plan also requires good players.

Taylor and I took one patrol of about 15 Lao militiamen—and along came the women, bringing cooking ware and extra food and ammo. So much for the ambush, I thought.

We moved out following the trail around the rice paddies, moving along, equipment clattering, people talking, geese squawking in the village.

We went maybe three or four miles when one of our forward scouts came running back and said the Pathet Lao were ahead not a kilometer away, walking toward us on the same path. There was no time to do anything.

I insisted that the women turn and hurry back to the village. They finally did so, but half the men went with them.

"No, Goddamnit," I called, trying to keep my voice low. "You men stay. Stay. Stay."

An interpreter hurriedly called something in Lao which I assumed meant "stay," and the women sat down.

"No, no, not the women," I said. "Tell the women to go."

The men heard the word "go" and again headed back for the village, followed by the women.

Taylor and I exchanged anguished looks. But we had to make the best of a situation that was rapidly deteriorating.

We quickly spread our force of seven or eight Laotions who remained with us and took up positions near the trail.

We heard the Pathet Lao coming: birds flew in alarm; twigs cracked; now and then we heard men talking in low voices, but clearly audible. Either they were careless . . . or maybe they wanted us to hear them. Then, without orders from Taylor or me, some of our men began firing wildly into the jungle.

"Jesus Christ" I muttered.

There was a stunned pause from the Pathet Lao, then return fire began cutting above us, sending leaves dancing around our heads.

We maintained a return fire for four or five minutes, but by then it was Taylor and me against the world, it seemed. We backed away, firing and throwing grenades.

As we pitched the last ones at them, Taylor shouted, "That'll set 'em on their asses for a little while." Then we broke away, running through the jungles, zig-zagging away from the village until we were clear of pursuers. An hour or so later we were back in the village. It wouldn't be the last time I would have to fight my way out of trouble because the Lao militia abandoned me.

ONE OF THE toughest soldiers I've ever known was Albert Slugocki, a Polish guy who never lost his accent. The first time I saw him was at the White Rose bar in Saraboury. Of course, it would be a while before I knew his name.

He was wearing a white satin suit and was sitting at a table with a gorgeous French girl. I was with several other guys and we were enjoying a weekend pass. I guess we were a bit rowdy at the bar because I glanced around once and Slugocki was glaring at us. I took my drink and went to the table. The girl flashed an engaging smile at me, which is more than I can say for Albert Slugocki. He was still glaring.

"I hope we're not too loud over there," I said, as a way of introduction.

Slugocki shrugged and said, "Your people are just up there showing their asses."

"Sorry," I said, "but I just had to come over and ask where you got that suit. It's a fantastic design. I like it."

Slugocki said he purchased it from a local tailor shop, then invited me to sit down. He introduced himself with his first name only, and vaguely explained that he worked for the government. The girl was a secretary with a French group that still operated in Laos, despite having been kicked out of neighboring Vietnam in 1954.

Slugocki never said what he did and he didn't ask me what I did. I personally did not believe he was with the American government, and suspected he might be a Soviet agent. In all honesty, with a couple of good glasses of bourbon under my belt and a beautiful French girl sitting beside me, I didn't give a rip about who he was.

I asked the girl if she cared to dance, and she looked at Slugocki, who nodded coolly in approval. After the song was over, I returned her to the table and Albert stood up and shook my hand.

"It was nice seeing you, Lionel," he said, with a look in his eye that told me it was time for me to leave. "Perhaps we'll meet again some day."

I bowed to the girl and kissed her hand, then, as I left, I leaned over to Albert and said, "Man, are you CIA or Russian, or what?"

He laughed and slapped me on the shoulder. "Nyet," he said, still laughing. Only later, much later, would I learn Albert was working in Southeast Asia with the CIA. In later months I would see him again.

16

Home Fires in Nam Tha

IN APRIL 1962, I took a patrol out in the boondocks and ran into a small force of Pathet Lao, who promptly shot the hell out of us and sent a good number of my men running. As I was getting out of the area, a grenade went off about ten yards or so away and sent a piece of shrapnel through my leg, hitting a blood vessel that ran like a flood. One of the women helped bind the leg and put on a pressure bandage. It got me a short stay at a hospital in Bangkok.

After the surgery, I came to and wanted a cigar . . . not only wanted one, I was begging for nicotine. There was no smoking in the ward. But a Marine from the U.S. Embassy heard of my plight and rigged up a long hose that ran from my window to the ground below. He attached the burning cigar at the exterior end, and let me have the other end. I was able to get a few good puffs off it, enough to satisfy my tobacco craving.

I was back in Laos in time to take part in an airborne operation. Somebody got the idea that maybe we could turn things around if we could train more Laotian Army guys to be paratroopers. We set up the training operation in a stretch of swamp-free ground and almost immediately ran into a problem. The troops would need boots when they hit the ground, otherwise it increased the risk of broken ankles and legs. So we hurriedly requested Army boots be shipped to us. They arrived quickly enough, but another problem arose. The Lao guys were so much smaller that none of the boots fit. We finally solved the dilemma by stuffing the boots with straw. The guys jumped all right, but as soon as they hit the ground and undid the harness, they all sat down and removed the boots, then replaced them with their traditional sandals.

In May 1962, some of the newly trained paratroopers joined the 55th Paratroop Battalion of the Lao Royal Army on a mission near Nam Tha, in the northwest corner of the country. The Pathet Lao had attacked the city and ran about 4,500 government troops off. We were to try to stem the drive of the enemy. I jumped with the battalion and for about a week we stayed in the area, fighting the Pathet Lao. There were small bands at first, then as the days went by, they grew larger. Before long we were in a desperate series of fire fights.

The extra training the paratroopers had received made them better soldiers than the regular militia guys, and they fought well. But soon the operation ended when we were ordered to withdraw.

"Home, sweet home," I said, as we arrived back at the old house. There was a warmth about the place. Often in the evenings we would gather around the grand piano, someone would try to play and we would sip beer and sing songs with attempted harmony, things like "Heart of My Heart," or "The Yellow Rose of Texas."

Somehow our real homes seemed a little closer when we played the old instrument, with its swayed keyboard. Such a glorious sound it made. The more I sang the more I relished the feel of the place, the bond of camaraderie. The piano brought us closer, helped braid us into a team, not only of fighting men, but of souls far from home.

But one day a large force of Pathet Lao came toward the village, and we knew we had to get out. We carried all our equipment and loaded it onto jeeps or carts or whatever we could find.

"What about the piano?" I asked. "Are we going to leave it?"

"Hell, no," Taylor said.

But we couldn't take it, Lt. Lunday said. It was too heavy and it was not military issue. The decision had already been made to burn the house, so the Communists could not make use of it. Someone played one last rendition of "Yellow Rose of Texas," and then we walked out. The piano was to stay inside. We poured gasoline on the house and touched it off. Then we stood in the gathering twilight, silently watching it crumble in the great rush of flames. The piano could be seen still standing. It was a sad moment for all of us. We were leaving something behind that had become a part of us. God knows how many people enjoyed a few moments of peace listening to the piano, or trying to play it.

I watched the piano until it crumbled in a burst of crackling coals. Then I turned and walked away.

Behind me I heard Taylor exclaim, "At least those bastards won't get to play it."

War not only kills the dreams of people, but it also destroys the things that help them make those dreams.

17

Delivering Babies for the Laotians

A LONG WITH BEING a combat soldier and paratrooper, I had been cross-trained as a medic. One day one of the pregnant wives trailing the Lao militia reached her time. I was hurriedly summoned to help. The woman, who was about 18, was a lovely thing with bright eyes and long dark hair. I called her Lani. Privately, I prayed for help, but outwardly I nodded and smiled, saying she was all right. It was her first child and I feared it might be a breech, but I think the girl was just too tense. I kept talking to her, forcing a laugh, and finally she seemed to ease up, and nature took its course. Out came the baby as healthy as could be, and I gave it the traditional pop on the butt to start him crying.

There was a hell of a lot of commotion after that, with old women running and shouting; I eased out of the hut, lit me a cigar and thought I might faint.

"Jesus," I said to Taylor, "I've been through a lot in my life, but I've never done anything like that before. It was a damn nice thing, you know?"

Taylor produced a bottle of bourbon, but I waved it away. "I think I'll go sit outside and watch the fireflies," I said.

Sitting by the stream, I spent an hour or more thinking about all of it. God, here we were over in some strange land helping kill people we thought were bad, and at the same time a new baby comes. I wondered if my being here was going to make his life any better for him when he grew up.

A week or so later there was some sort of little festivity welcoming the baby to the village. Lani appeared at the door of our house and asked for me.

"Choo," she said, smiling and bowing.

She said something in Lao, which I assumed was a thank-you. I bowed back and said, "You're welcome."

Within a few days another woman had a baby and I sat in on that one, although the women of the village seemed to be in control. This woman already had a couple of children. I doubted she needed anyone to assist. In all, I delivered eleven babies in Laos.

Having a little knowledge about maternity matters led to a serious problem for me, one that I feared would land me in the brig.

A sergeant and a captain, both from another Special Forces unit, came into the house raising hell. They were drunk and using vulgar language. I ignored them. But the officer, I'll call him Gordo, came to me and became quite contrite. He took off his boonie cap.

"Chief, you gotta do me a favor," he said, his voice almost sober. I thought he might want some money to get some more booze. "If it's money, sir, I'm busted."

He shook his head. Then:

"I got this girlfriend in the village. You know, we're pretty close. She's going to have a kid."

I winced. "Good God."

"Yeah, I know," he said, fumbling with the cap. "Well, since we'll be leaving one of these days and I won't be able to take her and take care of the baby, I was wondering if you could help her . . . help her have an abortion."

"An abortion." I stood up and got a cigar out of my pocket. "Hell, I don't know nothing about that. I can't do that. That's not something you expect to face in combat."

"Hell, Chief, you've delivered babies," Gordo pressed. "I've seen you holding the babies."

I glanced at him, then turned away. "That's different. That's helping a kid live. You're asking me to kill a living soul."

But Gordo was persistent. "She's still early. It's no big deal."

I shook my head and finally lit the cigar. "Well, it's a big deal to me. It goes against all my beliefs. We're over here to kill commies, not innocent babies."

He glared at me. Then he said, "Who the hell are you supposed to be, the pope or something? Since when have you been such a saint?"

"It's got nothing to do with me being a saint," I said. "I just don't believe in it. It's wrong. I won't do it."

"Bullshit," he snapped.

I recognized the glint in his eyes. And then he lunged at me, swinging wildly. I stepped back and one of the blows skipped off my forehead. Then I pushed him away.

"I'm not going to hit you because you're drunk," I yelled. "But if you don't sit down and behave, I'll deck you, sir."

He charged at me; I met it with a straight left jab to the chin and he went down. He started to get up and I hit him with a right; he stayed down.

Now, John, the sergeant, started shouting at me.

"You struck an officer," he said. "This is all bullshit, Pinn."

Then he took a swing at me. I blocked it and popped him hard on the jaw and he fell beside Gordo.

I took the cigar out of my mouth and walked outside. The two arose and shouted insults at me. I tried to ignore them and walk away, but the captain roared and tackled me from behind.

That did it. I got up and hit him hard, and he came back with a blow to my face. Then I hit him and he reeled backwards and slammed against the house. I don't remember much after that except I heard Taylor shouting at me to stop. Next thing I knew I was coming to in my bunk, the room and the world swirling about me. I didn't know what had happened. But Taylor told me I was giving the captain a sound thrashing.

"Only way we could stop you was to give you a shot of sodium pentathol," he said. "It knocked you out. We were afraid you would kill him."

I didn't see the captain again and I never knew for sure what happened to the woman and her baby.

It really angered me when I heard of women in occupied countries having to bear children fathered by Americans, young men who simply went home. But the abortion was just as bad, in my opinion.

18

River Doctor

IN MAY THE fighting continued to intensify as the Pathet Lao grew stronger. We stepped up our defensive measures around villages, placing mines and booby traps wired in the dense underbrush.

Royal Lao troops showed up from time to time to try to bolster the defense. One group was led by a colonel named Nu Pet, who apparently heard about my fight with the captain.

We were sitting by a campfire one evening having a few drinks and pondering our fate. The colonel joined us; he kept eyeing me. Then, grinning, he spoke, saying:

"Sergeant Pinn, you have to behave over here. You know you Americans are worth twenty-five thousand dollars."

"The hell you say," I said, trying to sound halfway polite.

"The enemy will pay that much if we deliver you to them," the colonel stated, still grinning.

"Dead or alive?" I asked. It was hard not to be sarcastic.

Nu Pet laughed again, nodding, as though the whole thing was a joke.

Someone began talking about women, which I believed to be a more suitable subject. But every so often the colonel would grin at me and say, "Yes, sir, Sergeant Pinn, you're worth twenty-five thousand. As you Americans say, twenty-five big ones."

His skin glistened from the sweat; the dancing flames gave his face an evil glow.

At least two more times that night the colonel mentioned the figure of $25,000, each time directing the message to me. After another drink, I walked to my quarters and impulsively grabbed my Tommy gun, rammed a magazine into it, then hurried back to the fire. The colonel had gone to his hut to retire for the night.

I hurried there and walked in just as he was lying down in his bunk. By then some of the other men, alarmed by my actions, ran in behind me.

But I put the gun right in the colonel's face and said, "You son-of-a-bitch, I'm going to blow your head off."

His eyes looked like they were going to pop out of his head. He was trying to speak but no words came. Taylor and some of the other guys were tugging at my arms, asking me to calm down and trying to take the gun away from his head.

"You gonna sell me out for twenty-five thousand, are you?" I said, delighting in the fear that flashed in his eyes. "You ain't gonna be around to collect!"

"Lionel, you'll ruin your career," one of the men said. Others were pulling at me . . . pulling very gently, afraid they might accidentally cause the weapon to discharge.

The colonel was sweating and whimpering softly, "It was no harm. It was no harm."

Finally I eased the barrel from his head and turned away. I walked out, calling a warning: "You ever say anything again about turning any of us over to those bastards, you'll be a dead man."

There was hell to pay the following day. The Laotians

reported the incident to U.S. officials, and before long a radio message came in from headquarters in Vientiane to relieve me of training duty.

At that point, Col. Simon had completed his tour and returned to the U.S. The man in charge was Col. Aito Keravouri, who, I was told, was highly displeased with my conduct, which, he said, had not only been a violation of military order, but also a breach of political etiquette.

Lt. Lunday, a slim, even-tempered man with a sense of humor, gave me the word and said I was to be reassigned as a medical specialist in another province. For the time being, I was told, I was to leave my Tommy gun. My only weapon would be a .38 caliber pistol.

Lunday added with a slight grin, "Try not to point it at anybody."

"Yeah, shit," I said. "I know. I fouled up. It was the damn firewater. I should know better."

I was sent to Luang Prabang Province to a village that lay along the Mekong River, which flowed southeast through Laos and formed the boundary along the border of Thailand, Cambodia, and Vietnam.

The government of Laos provided an interpreter whom I called Jimmy, who was to go with me to the villages. We rode in a Pagoda boat, a vessel with a small Buddhist altar erected on the stern, which gave it a spiritual aura as it came through the early morning fog.

I was called the "River Doctor." At each stop we would tie the boat to a tree and Jimmy would go ahead and introduce me to the villagers, asking them if they had any medical problems. The people would line up to see me, sometimes fifteen or twenty of them.

At night we would either sleep in the boat or bed down in one of the huts, enjoying a fish dinner with rice, or sometimes some fruit and vegetables. One of the first things I looked for when I would arrive in a new village was to see how many women were near the end of a pregnancy. While I had been involved in bringing babies into the world, it wasn't a task I relished.

In most cases I would pass out some aspirin or bandage some sores and cuts and give a little medicine for pinworms and ringworm. There was a profound need for a dentist and also a good supply of vitamins would have been a help.

In June 1962 a truce was called and political leaders from many nations met in Geneva to try to work out a settlement in the conflict. The war seemed about to end. Yet I was told to continue my mission of goodwill, aiding the poor villagers.

Laos was steamy even riding on the river; it was much worse during June and July; the only time there was relief was when a heavy rain fell, and thunderstorms would send down cooling air that hovered above the high slopes. One evening I rode out in the open, letting the rain hit my face. I took off my shirt and sang lustily the old folk song, "Oh, It Ain't Gonna Rain No More." Jimmy sat up front, guiding the boat, turning from time to time to laugh and shake his head at my singing.

We came to a village just as the rain diminished and the fleeting clouds revealed a glowering red sun sinking into the horizon. Jimmy alighted; I waited on the boat, enjoying a cigar. When he returned he announced that we would examine any ill villagers the next day. Meantime, there was no room in any of the huts we were told, so we would have to sleep on the boat.

"Uh-uh, not me," I said. "I've been on this damn thing all day. I'm getting off for a while."

Jimmy shrugged. "They say we stay on the boat."

"You can stay," I said. "I'm getting off."

I grabbed my medical kit, put on a shirt, and stode through the village, nodding at the people who sat outside their huts. Some returned the greeting, others simply stared at me, or stared beyond me. I found a nice grassy knoll overlooking the river and the village and sat against a tree, smoking a cigar and watching the fireflies glimmer in the gathering gloom of twilight.

It was a good night to sit quietly and do nothing. My thoughts drifted to home. My sons were growing up; I hadn't seen them in a while. Lionel Jr. would soon be a teenager. Kenneth was not far behind. But the marriage was finished, smashed like a ship on the rocks. Una had grown weary of being a soldier's wife.

Jimmy came up and even in the fading light I could see he was troubled about something.

"Sometimes I don't think a soldier should get married," I said, unaware that he could care less about my opinion.

"We have visitors," he said, his voice stiff.

I looked beyond him and saw a group of about ten men standing there . . . then I almost bit the cigar in two. They had rifles aimed at us. I stood up. "What the hell . . ."

Before I could finish one of the men barked out an order in Laotian. He talked for several seconds.

I knew it meant we were prisoners, but I didn't quite catch the rest.

"We are to go with them," Jimmy said. "They kill us if we try to run. OK?"

I nodded. "OK. Anything they say. No sweat."

A man with a red kerchief around his head removed my sidearm, then gave me a push to go back toward the village. But before entering, we turned north along a narrow trail.

In the darkness one of our captors made a hissing noise,

meaning we were to be quiet. It was July 16, 1962. It was my third capture. I had gotten away from the Japanese and the Chinese in WWII and Korea. I wondered what my chances would be this time. An American advisor here in the jungles could simply disappear and never be heard of again.

WE WALKED THROUGH most of the night, running some of the time. The people with the guns seemed to be in a hurry. Then, just as dawn was breaking, the leader of the group, a short, lean guy with thick dark hair and a trace of a mustache, stopped and came to me, speaking quickly.

"What's he saying?" I asked Jimmy.

The interpreter answered, "He say you are river doctor and their sergeant is ill. You must make him well or you will be executed."

"What's wrong with this sergeant?" I asked. "I know a little, but I'm not a miracle worker."

Jimmy relayed the question, but the man did not answer. He turned and we were again given a push to hurry along. At midmorning, hot and thirsty and just a little hungry, we arrived at a village where armed men roamed about in abundant numbers. This was a Pathet Lao stronghold. Our travel during the night had ended up once again along the banks of the Mekong. I was led to a hut where a man lay sprawled out on a mat. He was probably in his thirties or early forties, with several scars on his face and arms. Old fights, I thought. He was breathing rapidly, and his eyes flitted.

God, I thought. I hoped it wasn't typhoid or some exotic disease that was about to be a plague. I felt his forehead.

"Burning up with a fever," I said to Jimmy. "Maybe it's just some kind of flu or something. Let's hope."

The lead man of the group that captured us spoke again, shaking his AK-47 as he talked. I knew what he was saying, but Jimmy repeated it anyway.

"He say if you don't make well we both die," he said, his voice shaky.

I stared up at him and nodded. "Tell 'em not to sweat it. We'll take care of him."

The sick man, we were told, was a personal friend of the leader of the Communist forces in Laos, a fellow named Kong Le. Hence, the much-emphasized threat of death if I failed to cure him.

There was no way of knowing for sure what the problem might be, but I got two aspirins from my bag—actually it was the APC pill, an Army favorite that included aspirin—and asked for water. A young woman who apparently was the camp nurse got a cup of water and we forced the sergeant to drink it and take the pills.

Then, over my shoulder, I told Jimmy, "Tell them I need some help. We gotta carry this bastard and put him in the water."

Jimmy was clearly distressed by this, but repeated the message.

The Pathet Lao guy with the AK-47 glared at me and raised an objection.

"They think you might drown him," Jimmy said.

"Hell, do they think I'm that stupid?" I asked. "Tell the dumb son-of-a-bitch that the cool water will help bring down the fever and he'll feel better. I don't know what else to do."

Finally, after some more debate, the guy issued some orders and three of the other men leaned down and lifted the sergeant. I walked out ahead and waved for them to follow.

By the time we got to the water's edge there were forty or

fifty people and I waded into the river and told them to hand me the patient.

There wasn't a sound as I took the guy and dipped him down in the water, taking care to keep his head above the surface. He was shaking, his teeth chattering, but I smiled reassuringly at the hostile, suspicious group which encircled me.

Since none of them could speak English, I said, "This old bastard is too mean to die. I'd love to drown him, but not today. It's OK. No sweat."

After several minutes in the water, I gestured for help, and we lifted him back out, then took him back to his hut.

I never did know whether it was luck, or the APC, or the water, or a combination of factors, but within a half hour the sergeant's fever broke, he sat up and smiled weakly at his comrades, and later asked for something cool to drink. By that evening he was calling for food.

The Pathet Lao said I cured him. One of them even slapped me on the back and produced a bottle of liquor, urging me to drink. I shook my head no, but the man insisted. By then the others had circled around me, smiling and nodding in approval. I finally took one drink.

It turned out that one of the men in the group spoke some English, and the girl, the one who had some medical knowledge, spoke it even better. They told me I was to stay in their village and help with the other sick people.

It was an awkward moment. Technically, I was not a POW, because America was not at war with these people of Laos. But the reality of the situation was that I was very much a prisoner, and they were an enemy. Yet, at the same time, they couldn't care less about the Geneva Convention, and the fair treatment of captives. I looked over at Jimmy who sat with a pained expression on his face. The point the Pathet Lao were making was that I had all the interpreters I needed here. There was no need to keep him.

"I have to have my man who helps me care for the sick," I told the girl. She relayed the message to the others, some of whom still kept their rifles slung over their shoulders. There was some talk, then the girl said, "He is an enemy of the people."

"Aw, bullshit," I said. "He helps me take care of the sick. He helps me. You cannot harm him. He is a prisoner."

There was more talk, then two of the men pointed their weapons at me and others took me by the arms and led me to a hut. There, I saw an old blanket on the floor. The men indicated they would be outside, guarding me.

A little later I heard Jimmy talking loudly. Then the talking stopped. The night settled to the buzzing of the insects in the jungles. I sat on the floor and waited. A few minutes later I heard several shots. They were slow, deliberate. One, then another, then several seconds later, a third one. I knew Jimmy had died for his country.

FOR THE NEXT two days I was hustled around the village and to nearby villages to care for the sick, mostly the men who had been wounded in skirmishes with the government troops. But there were also children and elderly who looked up at me with great hope in their eyes. Some of them had learned to say the words, "river doctor help."

As I saw the sick, I was constantly under guard by two or three Pathet Lao troops who were armed with rifles. At least one would have his weapon trained on me at all times. My mind was clicking along looking for a way to make a break.

Then, on the third day, the girl who spoke English came to the hut and said I was to go north several kilometers to treat the sick in another village. Suddenly, it dawned on me that if I didn't get away now, I might never. There was only one way to do it, without anyone getting hurt.

I held up my medical bag for the girl to see, turned it upside down, and nothing came out.

"I'm out of everything," I said. "I can't help anyone without medicine and bandages. The only thing I can do is go back and get more supplies and bring them back."

It was a long shot, maybe even a little stupid, but it was my only chance.

She looked at me with great suspicion, but then relayed my comments to the guard. There was some excited talking and shouting; finally the sergeant that I had helped cure entered the hut. He listened to the situation, glanced at me a few times, with his watery, bloodshot eyes that looked like two pissholes in the snow, then nodded gravely.

The sergeant had been helping his recovery process by drinking liquor; his solemn demeanor was probably the result of too much alcohol rather than despairing over medical shortages. Then, he spoke, his words halting and slurred, pausing for long moments. The others stood by obediently, awaiting his decision. Finally, the girl turned to me:

"You pledge your word to return when you find supplies?"

"I do," I said quickly, flabbergasted that they were even thinking about trusting me.

The girl studied my face closely. "We have many sick people," she said. "You Americans can help us."

I nodded. "These villagers are not my enemy," I said. "I want to be able to help them. I'll return with supplies."

The girl didn't look like a revolutionary. She was with the Pathet Lao, but she was concerned about her people.

"We will await your return," she said, her voice icy. Then she left the hut.

Three Pathet Lao soldiers escorted me to the river, climbed into a small motorboat, then took me down the Mekong, pausing from time to time at villages. They would talk for a moment, study the village to determine if there were government troops, then gun the motor and speed off.

Finally we came to an area where it was certain government forces were patrolling, and the motor was put on idle as we neared the bank.

The three men put their weapons down on the bottom of the boat so they would not be seen. They said nothing as I jumped out. Then they were gone.

19

An Uncertain Peace

I COULDN'T BELIEVE that they would be so naive as to think I would return to captivity. At the same time I felt drawn to the innocent simplicity of the villagers who had trusted me. Inside me, there was a strange yearning that somehow I should go back. I watched them fade into the muggy green heat of the delta, then turned to seek some friendly forces.

A government patrol soon appeared, questioned me briefly, then radioed to their headquarters. In less than an hour a helicopter arrived and I ducked and trotted toward it. It had been incredibly easy. But at the same time I realized how lucky I had been. They could have shot me just as they did Jimmy.

I got back to a village where a White Star team was quartered, was summoned to the shack where there was a radio set up, and got a summary butt-chewing by a staff officer with Col. Keravouri.

"Why didn't you check in?" he asked. "You've been gone three days."

"Captured," I said. "Damn Pathet Lao got me. They killed my interpreter."

After that I was told to report back to the old outfit in Saraboury. When I returned I wanted to get my Tommy gun back and go find Col. Nu Pet. I felt he was somehow behind my capture. But I was reigned in. I never did see him, but I've always wondered if he got $25,000.

"I should have shot the son-of-a-bitch when I had the chance," I told Taylor, who nodded solemnly.

Our new operations were in another village not far from the city of Saraboury. The cease-fire seemed to be holding. Taylor and I went into the city a few times on Saturday nights and drank enough whisky to float a barge.

We sang songs, occasionally got into fights, and talked about serious subjects like using manure on crops, the wisdom of some dogs, and the high cost of funerals. I always figured on being buried at Arlington with my Dad. For his money, Taylor said, he'd just as soon be cremated and the ashes thrown to the four winds.

Finally, the time came for us to pack it up and go home. The war in Laos was over, we were told. The government and the Pathet Lao had agreed to a coalition neutrality, which I assumed meant there would be fair elections.

I'm not sure about the elections, but it did not in the end mean neutrality. For in the years to come Communist North Vietnam would use Laos as a safe zone in which to stockpile supplies for their war with South Vietnam. Of course, America supported the South. I would one day go there and once again see the Mekong River and once again return to Laos. But that was down the road.

20

Back to the States

WE CAME BACK to the U.S. in September 1962, a time when all attention was on the University of Mississippi where a black Air Force veteran, James Meredith, was trying to be admitted. The Kennedy administration had sent troops to Oxford, Mississippi, to ensure he was registered.

The civil rights movement and the simmering Cold War brought great change to America. In 1962 when I returned from Laos, we were on the brink of nuclear war with the Soviet Union over missiles in Cuba.

No wonder not many people paid attention to the little mess in Laos and what was happening in South Vietnam.

I went back to Fort Bragg, North Carolina, where I became a physical education instructor for Special Forces trainees. I ran them ragged, egging them on by puffing on a cigar and keeping in stride with them by running backwards.

Now thirty-nine years old, my old body was about as good as ever, but my eyesight left a little to be desired. An Army doctor said I needed glasses.

I got a pair of dark-rimmed ones which friends said made me look scholarly. One week I had some time off so a few of the older sergeants decided to go to New York. We wore our Special Forces uniforms which included, of course, the green berets.

One day we went to an upscale restaurant for lunch and the man at the front desk said we could not go in without reservations. But another man, the boss apparently, recognized us as Green Berets and found us a table.

We had just sat down when I noticed a striking, dark-haired woman at a table across the room. Jackie Kennedy, I thought.

"Good God, there's Mrs. Kennedy," I said, "the First Lady." I wanted to say hello to her, but the other guys kept telling me to sit still and not make a scene.

But finally the heart won and I stood up and went to her table and introduced myself.

She offered her hand, then laughed slightly. "You resemble a friend of ours," she said.

"Me? Who do I look like?"

"Aristotle Onassis," she said. Then she said to her friends, "Doesn't he? With those dark-rimmed glasses?"

We talked for only a moment. I told her I was from Brookline, the area where her husband was from. And we talked briefly about Laos. Then I gave her my green beret. "Keep it as a memento," I said.

She smiled, then handed me a coin. "You keep this," she said. It was a Club 21 coin. I still have it.

When President Kennedy was assassinated in Dallas on Nov. 22, 1963, I was still at Fort Bragg. I halted the training session I had. I went to my room in the barracks, took the coin and sat on my bunk, staring at it. I wept like a baby.

Years later, when she became a book editor, I called her at Doubleday, and she remembered me. "Why, Lionel," she said, "when are you going to write a book?"

"When I can collect enough to write about," I said.

21

Training Cubans

IN OCTOBER 1963, I was awarded the Combat Infantryman Badge for the third time for my service in Laos. It meant twin silver stars would sit atop the blue badge. I didn't think too much about it at the time. But in later years it would mean something special. Through most of 1963 and into 1964 I was busy training the new guys coming into Special Forces at Fort Bragg. There were a lot of volunteers. I did have one break in the training, however.

In the spring of 1963 I was one day summoned to the company orderly room where a captain wanted to see me. I didn't know the man, had never seen him before.

He shook hands and said, "I'm told you've been cross-trained as a medic."

I nodded. "Yes, sir. I hope you don't have any babies to be delivered."

He shook his head and grinned, "Not likely. But there is a special operation that might be of interest to you. Would you like to be in on it?"

"I think so," I said. "What is it?"

He wouldn't tell, but he told me to report to a site called Camp McCall, an out-of-the-way part of Fort Bragg. I was told to wear a new uniform: Levis, a long sleeve shirt, a ball cap, and tennis shoes.

The mission, it turned out, was to train Cuban exiles to make night parachute jumps. They wanted me along because they needed someone with some medical training. They also had some body bags in case things really got bad. The captain in charge was close-mouthed about it. But I had the distinct feeling this thing was going to end up with a drop into Cuba with the idea of taking out Fidel Castro.

We trained, and made jumps successfully, but for some reason the mission never came off. At least not that I know of. After several months I went back to heading the physical training, which meant running and running and running. I loved it. And sometimes I would smoke a cigar and run backwards, just to show them that a guy over 40 could hold his own with them. God, they were good men. They were the Army's best, good soldiers who wanted to be better soldiers. Most, I think, were a lot like me, in that they believed we could make things better in Vietnam by fighting and defeating the communists.

22

The Reason Una Left

TRAINING TROOPS IS an OK job, but I began to get an itch to go to Vietnam. When you're a soldier and there is a war going on somewhere, you feel you have to be there. It's not that I enjoyed killing enemy soldiers, or witnessing the suffering of the civilian people and seeing the horrific things that go with it, it's just that if it's going to take place, then it was where I needed to be. For a professional soldier, war can sometimes be an escape from the things that are not going right in his personal life.

I had been married three or four times and I was spending more and more time worrying about those failures. Many of the problems had been my fault. I had done some truly dumb things.

There are some people—me included—who always seem to get caught at things they're not supposed to be doing. The most striking example of this took place when I was on temporary duty in Florida and my wife, Una, went with me, renting a small apartment.

On New Year's night several of the guys were going to go with me to the Orange Bowl. We had planned for it earlier and obtained tickets. We had met some young women who had worked at a nightclub and they were going with us. We had somehow come up with eight tickets.

After pulling duty that day we changed into civilian clothes—stashed away for emergency situations—and got ready to go.

About that time I said, "I gotta call home and tell my wife something. What can I tell her?"

One of the guys, we called him "Big George," suggested, "Just tell her we're going fishing."

So we went to the game, drank and partied and made fools of ourselves, then laughed our way into a club for a late dinner and more drinks. About 1 a.m. I worriedly told the guys, "I got to get out of here. My wife will kill me."

And Big George says, "My wife's about five-two and weighs just over a hundred and ten pounds. But she can beat the hell out of me when she gets mad. So I gotta go home and own up to it. You guys might as well do the same."

I didn't like that idea. I figured I could outsmart Una. So I stopped at a market and bought some fresh fish. When I got to the apartment, she was waiting up for me.

"Look at the fish I caught," I said. "Pretty nice, huh?"

"Oh, you caught some fish, huh?" she said, her voice cold. "Where'd you catch 'em, on the sidelines?"

I tried to stay cool. "The what?"

"You jackass," she shouted. "I saw you on the TV. You and your buddies and some floozies. The camera was on you for five seconds. And I said, 'There's my great husband.'"

I was dumbfounded; I couldn't think of a thing to say. I'd been caught red-handed.

Finally, I said, "We were on TV?"

Then she started laughing. Now what? She was standing over the sink, looking at the fish.

"I knew you were not so bright, but this is even bad for you," Una said. "Look."

I glanced down at the fish. On each of them was a blue stamp that read "Inspected by Federal Government." Not long after that we divorced.

23

Vietnam

I FIXED MY mind on getting into the new war that was slowly unfolding in Vietnam. Casualties were light by most standards: One American killed drew headlines in many newspapers.

"Another Yank Killed in S. Viet."

Then it was two or three. Then more.

The Army wasn't ready to send me anywhere, making me stick to training new members of the Green Berets. Finally, in 1965, at age 42, I retired. I had been in for twenty-five years, and figured it was time to hang it up.

I was now over 210 pounds, a real heavyweight, so I went to Las Vegas and got a job as a bouncer in a nightclub. It wasn't a bad way to earn a living. You got to meet a lot of interesting women . . . interesting and good looking. Actually, I wasn't called a bouncer, but rather part of hotel security.

When Frank Sinatra came to town, which was often, I was part of the security, and in fact, once was the main guy with him. He was tough for his size. I don't mean we fought, but his bearing was tough. One evening before a performance he told me he was ready to order something to eat, telling me what to have sent up to the room.

Then he said, "And get yourself something, too. And I don't

mean a sandwich, I mean a real full-course meal. Tell 'em if you don't eat, I don't sing."

Meantime the war in Vietnam really began to break open. In November 1965 the 1st Cavalry Division ran into a North Vietnamese ambush at the Ia Drang Valley, and the unit suffered more than 400 casualties.

In early 1966 I received a telegram from the Department of Defense signed by Robert McNamara, the Secretary of Defense. The Army was desperately short of seasoned non-commissioned officers—sergeants, like me—in Vietnam and needed help. I was offered a chance to be assigned to the 4th Infantry Division in Vietnam. I wanted to go over with the Green Berets, but decided I'd take what I could get. There was a war on. I wanted to be in it.

I hadn't been part of the regular Army—common soldiers—for some years and knew I would have to make some adjustments. No, I wouldn't. Some of the young soldiers, the draftees, were going to have to make some adjustments for me.

The Army put me on a plane and a day later I was in Saigon, processing through Military Assistance Command Vietnam (MACV). Vietnam was different from Laos, a bit more upscale. The city had a modern downtown area with lots of bicycle traffic.

I was assigned to the headquarters company of the 4th Division, commanded by Gen. William Peers. Eventually I became the first sergeant, meaning I was the top NCO in the division. The 4th was operating in the Central Highlands. I started sensing some problems right away. The soldiers, the young Americans, tried hard, they tried damn hard, but there just wasn't the right spirit there. They sensed, I think, that there was no winning solution here, that the politics were all wrong.

More than anything, being with the 4th showed me that I was getting old. These guys were not fighting men, they were kids. I couldn't believe that I had once looked something like that. The soldiers who were with me in Korea, with the 2nd Infantry Division, had seemed more mature. But they were probably the same. It was me getting older, trying to be the perfect soldier. Most of these boys didn't care about a Combat Infantryman Badge . . . they just wanted to go home.

One of the things about Vietnam that was different from the others was the measure of distance. In Vietnam we talked about "klicks" which means kilometers, or we talked about meters; in Korea we talked about yards and miles; during World War II in the jungles of New Guinea and the Philippines, it was often a matter of feet and even inches.

Helicopters made this war different from Korea or World War II. We would mount up on choppers, the big Hueys, and head off on a "search and destroy" mission, find the enemy, fight, then pull back to our base camp near Plieku. Then we would come back—those who weren't killed or wounded badly—and eat, sometimes even have a beer, then sleep in a bunk.

Most of the time I would remain at the division headquarters, keeping up with casualties and filling out reports. But sometimes I'd throw a magazine into the Tommy gun, check out a few grenades, and ride with these kids. We'd storm in like the cavalry, swooping down on a village where the Viet Cong or the North Vietnamese troops were thought to be, trade fire, then come home.

It became routine. One day we moved out early in the morning, just as the sun rose. I sat out on the edge of the landing skids, cradling the Tommy gun close to my chest, watching the thick green jungle pass below me, keeping an eye out for North

Vietnamese or Viet Cong. (The only way to tell the latter group was if they started shooting at us).

There were about fifteen helicopters and we roared along, sort of skimming the treetops. From time to time we would rush over an open plain. One of them was to be our landing zone, an area where intelligence had reported VC and NVA activity.

Just then a gunner on the helicopter yelled to me and gestured. A grassy plain about the size of a couple of football fields loomed ahead. The LZ. I raised my fist and jerked my arm up and down twice, meaning for the men to get ready.

Suddenly I felt a terrific impact, a jolt, and the chopper bolted and shuddered as though it had hit an invisible brick wall.

My God, I thought, we're hit and we're going to all die here. We're going down in flames!

At the same time I saw below me puffs of smoke coming from the jungle, the telltale sign of weapons being fired, but it was as though I was seeing something in a dream or a vision. This really couldn't be happening. The noise of the helicopters obscured the sounds.

My mind came back into focus. The adrenaline was racing, a call to action. I had to do something. My immediate concern was the chopper. It started lurching to the right, raising my side up higher. WHOOMPF! In a flash the thing burst into flames. I heard some of the boys screaming inside, the sound rising above the roar of the blast and the high-pitched scream of the engine.

We'd been hit by a rocket and the fire was starting to scorch my neck and arms. We were spinning crazily and I saw the trees and the grass below. I jumped. I didn't think about it, I just jumped.

Next thing I knew I was crashing through the small limbs and branches of a tree, then I was flat on my back on the ground. For a moment I couldn't move and I was sure the burning chopper was going to land right on top of me. But then I saw it careening off to my right, followed by a heavy banging sound as it struck the earth. I saw the black smoke rising and then heard a distinct explosion. I knew the boys inside all were dead. I hoped it had been quick for them.

It was a nightmarish scene, absolute chaos:

The chopper burning, gunfire erupting all around me, bullets ripping the leaves in the underbrush, men running crazily, shouting and waving their arms, some of them falling, some standing as though in shock.

I managed to get up, apparently suffering nothing more than some bad scratches and a puncture wound. Cringing and hunched over, I ran toward the chopper, hoping somehow there was something I could do. But the fire was too intense. Some of the other Hueys had landed by then and men with fire extinguishers ran forward. It was all for nothing. I sat down and watched. Only one other man survived. The pilot and gunner and about ten of my men were lost.

A medic came up and started putting bandages on my head and arms. I had been cut badly but didn't feel the pain. By now we were under fire from the North Vietnamese troops who certainly seemed to know where we were planning to land.

Their shots were whizzing by and popping into a muddy bank of a ravine where we had sought cover.

I retrieved my Tommy gun and began firing, the hammering sound somehow distant. I kept looking toward the smoldering ruins of the chopper, my mind on the poor souls.

"What the hell are we doing here?" I shouted.

The other boys, their faces taut, eyes intense, took up cover along the ravine, looking toward me for some guidance.

I fired another burst, then turned to them and shouted, "These bastards are nothing compared to the Japs and Red Chinese. You should have been with me back then."

It was phony, but I had to try to boost their morale, try to tell them about a REAL war. But the sight of that helicopter crashing, burning and then exploding — with most of our guys still inside — was an unnerving thing to behold. It was unnerving even for an old pro like me. In case the boys didn't know it, we were in a REAL war.

They began firing into the jungles, their M-16s chattering with a steady rythm, but as I gazed down the line I saw some of them lying flat and simply holding their damn weapons up above their heads and shooting at air. I scrambled down the line and hit some kid on his butt.

"Don't waste bullets," I said. "Look at what you're shooting at."

"Hell," the lad replied, "I ain't getting my head shot off."

"The bastards can have this real estate," another shouted.

Draftees, I thought. I crawled away, then rose up and fired. I didn't see anybody, but I could tell where the fire was coming from. Then I ducked, rolled a few yards — pardon me, meters — then rose back up. An NVA soldier was running from tree to tree to get a flanking position on us. Two others galloped behind him.

"Hey, you," I said, calling to the private who didn't want to put his head above the ravine. "Crawl down here and come with me."

He hesitated, then came chugging along on hands and knees.

"Follow me."

"Where are we going?"

I stopped and turned. "Some of them bastards are moving around to the right. If they get down to the far end of this ditch they'll fire right down our throats. They'll shoot our asses off."

"Whatta we supposed to do, Sarge?"

I kept crawling, with him behind me. Over my shoulder I called, "We'll shoot their asses off first."

The ravine was full of thick grass with bare patches on the moist, reddish clay banks. It generally ran east and west, although there were curves in it. We had gone about twenty meters, when I heard or felt — I'm not sure which it was — something ahead. I put a hand back, then hissed, "Get ready."

"Oh, God," the kid moaned.

I turned and got on top of him, one knee holding him flat.

"Shoot when I shoot," I whispered.

He put his M-16 almost flat on the ground and pointed it down the ravine. I held my Tommy gun just about a foot above his head. Then, from the higher grasses in the field, I saw two, three figures roll into the ditch and start moving toward us. They were no more than ten meters away.

"Shoot!" I screamed, squeezing the trigger of my weapon. It lurched upwards slightly.

The kid below me opened up. I saw a pattern of red holes snake up the chest and face of the first NVA; the second one just seemed to get belted backward, and the third one's face literally disappeared in a burst of blood. All three quivered about on the ground.

"Get your ass up," I said, and raised up, taking my knee off the kid's back. I held the Tommy gun in my right hand and pulled him up with my left.

"Shoot over that way," I said.

We poured a stream of fire into a clump of nearby trees and heard a rewarding scream as two more NVA soldiers fell. The rest of them pulled away.

Now more of our choppers began drifting in, belching green men who hit the ground and sprinted in all directions. The firefight was over. Now we had to secure the area then care for our wounded and account for our dead.

This was the part that wasn't much different from Korea or World War II. I walked over to the melted remains of the helicopter. A lieutenant, noticing my bandages, came to me and asked how I was.

"I'm OK," I said, "but we got to get the names of those boys in the mess here. We have to carry them KIA."

"Excuse me, sergeant, but we'll carry them as missing in action, not killed," said the lieutenant.

I glared at him. "Sir, they're all dead in there."

"Sergeant, there's not enough left in there to scrape together one body to send back," the lieutenant said. "You want to go in there and try to put together one body? The only way to do it is report all of them MIA then later we can write a letter that they were aboard a craft that went down and all are presumed dead. That's the way it is."

I couldn't raise a good argument. It would have been impossible to separate the grisly remains and try to identify who was who.

24

In a Spirit World

WHILE WITH THE 4th Infantry Division, I kept sending in requests for transfer to the Special Forces. The 4th was a fine unit, but it was the regular Army, filled with what I called "common soldiers." I wanted to be with the Green Berets, because I was one of them. They were the uncommon.

One day I was walking outside and saw a Green Beret captain walking toward me. I wondered what he was doing in our area.

"Excuse me," he said, "but aren't you Sergeant Pinn?"

"Yes, sir," I said, popping a salute. "Can I help you, sir?"

"No, I was just in the area and I noticed your Special Forces patch," he said. "I'm Jim Morris. I wanted to meet you. I'd heard a lot about you at Fort Bragg."

I shrugged. "I helped train a lot of men."

Then he asked, "How do you like being in the 4th?"

"Good outfit," I said loudly. Then, glancing around so I wouldn't be overheard, I said in a lower voice: "Sir, I've been trying to get back into Special Forces for the longest time."

Morris nodded and said he'd pass the word along. A few days later the same thing happened. I saw this SF guy walking toward me and it turned out to be Sgt. Albert Slugocki, the mysterious man I had met in Laos.

"What the hell are you doing in a leg outfit?" he asked.

I told Albert the same thing I had told Jim Morris: I wanted back in the Special Forces.

In December 1967 the Army approved my request for transfer to the Green Berets; I cleared out my belongings from the 4th Division and caught a ride on a chopper from Pleiku to Kontum, headquarters of the 5th Special Forces. I was assigned to Command Control Central, CCC for short, and felt that I had at last returned home. It had been many long months away from the unit. In short order, the war changed in many ways, not only for me, but for all of us. The Communist forces launched their Tet offensive in February 1968 and the impact on our troops was dramatic. There seemed to be a sense among the regular Army units that we were not going to win after all, that indeed, we might be the bad guys. You could sense the morale slipping; discipline problems seemed to increase; I began hearing the first talk among other non-coms about "fragging" incidents.

I don't think it had that kind of an effect on the SF guys. We were as gung-ho as ever. I volunteered for missions behind the lines, some of them into adjoining Laos and Cambodia.

Early in March 1968 I went on a classified operation into Laos. There were three of us SF members, plus nine Vietnamese men who were on our payroll. Ever since Laos I had a hard time trusting the indigenous personnel. I just didn't trust them. The ones in Vietnam were no different.

We went in early on the morning of March 4, 1968, riding just above the treelines, cutting about 100 klicks into Laos. The mission was to capture a North Vietnamese colonel who was a ranking member of the enemy intelligence, or so we were told.

We thought we could get in quietly, set up an ambush, and then stop a small convoy and nab him.

But things went wrong from the first moment. The chopper set us down in a grassy knob with some small trees and brush, and as soon as it had departed over the treeline the nine Vietnamese guys melted away.

Almost instantly we were taken under fire by about fifteen or twenty men with automatic weapons. "We've been set up," I yelled. We rolled and tumbled down the shallow defile and tried to get cover, but the firing came from around us. "Let's get the hell out of here."

There wasn't much debate about that. We all got out grenades, then tossed them on the count of three. As soon as they exploded, we jumped up and ran as hard as we could, firing as we did. There was a clump of larger trees, about fifty or sixty yards away, and when we got there, our concentrated fire had cut down many of the North Vietnamese soldiers who had gotten to within ten yards of us.

Now it was Custer's Last Stand all over. . . . The bad guys kept up their heavy fire, shouting insults and shooting grenades at us with a rifle launcher. The things were exploding just a few yards away. By then we put out a radio distress call, a "Prairie Fire" signal, meaning we were in a lot of trouble and needed to be extricated. We needed a chopper, we needed Air Force jets to come in and strafe and bomb to help us, otherwise we were done for.

As I fired the Tommy gun, I kept praying, "Lord, don't leave me now."

Just then something hit me in the left side, sort of toward the back above the buttocks. At first I didn't feel anything, it just knocked me down and I felt myself tumbling on the damp ground. I opened my eyes in surprise and saw blue sky above.

And then everything changed. I was in the air floating above, and looking down. I saw myself lying there, blood oozing through my shirt and onto the ground. It was turning red. My eyes were closed and my face looked pale. I'm dead, I thought. I'm dead and I'm going to Heaven. I was at peace. It was beautiful. I watched my buddies alone firing at the circle of North Vietnamese soldiers who were working their way in.

"Chooch, hang in there, we got help on the way!" they shouted.

"Huh?" I opened my eyes and once again I was looking up at the blue sky. My side hurt, and my vision started getting blurred. "Oh, God, I'm dying," I said. "We gotta get out of here."

The sound of the firing grew loud again. And the sun was streaming down throught the tree limbs right into my face, hot and sickening. Someone gave me a shot.

The morphine kicked in, and I lay there, laughing at the trees. Was I going to die here?

"Pinn, you old bastard," I said to myself, "God is getting tired of saving your ass. Maybe it's time to hang it up."

I was vaguely aware of a helicopter hovering above us and a medic looking at my wounds.

"Oh, Jesus," he said. "It's one of them Chinese grenades, a B-40. The damn thing is stuck in his side."

I started to laugh again, a live grenade, unexploded, was stuck in my side. If it worked out and the handle engaged, it would blow me to hell and back. I was laughing, but even under the influence of the morphine, the drama of the situation was not lost to me. My life was at stake.

They put me on the chopper, very carefully. And then we were airborne.

In all the noise of a helicopter, casual talk is difficult. But I could see the medic telling the pilot what the problem was, because the guy turned around and looked at me with an expression of pure horror. "Jesus Christ," he said. I didn't hear him, but I could see the words formed by his mouth.

And then he said some other things that appeared to be, "If I had known he had a damned grenade stuck in him, I wouldn't have come."

I laughed again and called out, "Tell that bastard to cut off his radio. The waves could set this thing off."

When the message was relayed, the pilot again glared at me. I think if I had not been in such bad shape, he might have shot me. But in an hour we were landing at the 18th Evac Hospital at Pleiku. They knocked me out and when I came to, it was night. I was in no pain, and the grenade was gone. The brave surgeons had placed a heavy metal bracket around the thing and very gingerly removed it, keeping the handle down. A demolitions expert had taken it out and thrown it. They say it exploded in about two seconds. It was damn close.

Later someone got me a cigar and some whisky and I pondered what had happened. We were lucky to get out alive, all of us. I thought about the so-called "out-of-body" experience. I had heard of such things before, but I hadn't really believed. Maybe the Lord was telling me something. Maybe it was time to get out of combat and stay out. Seven Purple Hearts was enough for any man.

I stayed at the hospital for several weeks, and the life got on my nerves. The ward was full of young enlisted men who had been shot up in Vietnam, or hurt in accidents. Some, I figured, may have shot themselves.

And I started to see some of the cases of so-called post-traumatic stress disorder, which was a term that was coined in the Vietnam War.

When I began feeling better, I soon returned to the role of being a sergeant. A lot of the men could get up and move about with ease, and spent a lot of time just shooting the bull, making wise remarks. So I pulled rank on them. If they could get up and walk about, they could do some work. All I asked was that they police up the ward. Some of them didn't like it, but I couldn't stand seeing candy wrappers, cigarette packs, and empty cans lying around. I made them pick things up. It ruffled some of them. However, they had no choice. They might have been wounded, but they were still soldiers, as far as I was concerned.

One afternoon Captain Jim Morris came by. He was a young officer who had seen me one day at the 4th Infantry Division headquarters. He had been hit while on a mission. It was his fourth or fifth Purple Heart. He chuckled at the sight of the men picking up trash and sprucing up the place.

"Sergeant, I'm glad I'm an officer, or you'd have me doing that, too," he said.

I shrugged. "I think it's good for them to have something to do. I think it's a psychological boost to know we believe they're getting better."

Privately, I worried about the guys with the PTSD. I don't know if I believed in that stuff or not. Some guys did suffer so-called shell shock. But many of them did not. I think Gen. Patton was right. In a lot of cases, it was a means of getting out of combat duty . . . some of them were just plain cowards.

25

Last Call: 1968-1969

ONE OF MY favorite officers was Capt. Edward R. Lesesne, a 27-year-old career soldier who had spent five years as an enlisted man. Lesesne was commander of Recon Company of the 5th Special Forces and probably had more behind-the-lines missions under his belt than any other soldier in Vietnam.

He was not only a bright and caring soldier, he had one hell of a sense of humor. I detected this side of him one day when I lost what humor I had.

We were in our base camp, called FOB No. 2, at Kontum, and I was walking through the area. The Vietnamese men who worked with us liked to ride the little three-wheel motorcycles, or scooters, and would come roaring throught the camp at top speed, laughing and chortling.

One day I saw one coming down the lane between our quarters, and I just stood there, a grouchy look on my face. The poor guy driving it was carrying at least six comrades on the thing, piled behind him and on the fenders. He couldn't stop.

I saw the look of horror on his face; his eyes were wide with surprise and a sense of fear. Anyway, I reached down, grabbed the handle bars, and lifted the damn thing backwards. I heard a chorus of yells and screams and the group tumbled to the ground, kicking up a swirl of reddish dust.

"I'm tired of these damn things running wild," I announced loudly, as the group collected themselves from the turf.

For a moment I thought I might have to fight some of them, but then I heard this loud laughter, and there stood Capt. Lesesne, his head thrown back, his eyes sparkling.

"That was worth seeing again," he said, clapping his hands.

The young Vietnamese guys forced grins, gathered up their three wheeler, and quietly departed.

Lesesne slapped me on the back and invited me to have a beer with him sometimes, at the club. The club was our hangout, a frame building held together with scrap metal and a tin roof. The inside was crammed with chairs and tables, a bar, a juke box, and a few games, such as pinball.

There was a major—I'll call him Hornblower—who was not particularly well liked by anyone. In fact, if you ever watched the TV show M*A*S*H, this major would have been like Maj. Frank Burns.

He rarely took part in any combat duty and had the annoying habit of scratching his behind, often for rather long periods of time. Lesesne had one of the men keep a camera handy to try to record a scratching event. The man got the picture and Lesesne had it blown up to poster size, then had it mounted on the wall of the club.

Maj. Hornblower came in one night and saw it and raised a fuss. Then he sat at a table and ordered a drink. Lesesne and some of the other men finished their drinks, then a couple of them eased out the door. Outside, they found some brickbats and other heavy rocks, about the size of a softball, then hurled them into the air. The rocks and bricks came down on the tin roof with a roaring, crashing sound.

It made such a sudden racket that it sounded like handgrenades or mortar shells exploding. Someone inside yelled "Incoming!"

In that instant, Maj. Hornblower dove under the table, holding his hands over his head. The rest of the patrons, aware of the joke, roared with laughter. The rock-throwers hurried into the night and heard the results of their "attack" later.

Late in 1968 and early '69 the Green Berets teamed up with comando groups from the other branches of the service, such as the Navy SEALs, and formed what was known as SOG—an acronym for a unit known as the Studies and Observation Group. It sounded almost academic, but in reality it was an effort to intensify and streamline our combat intelligence-gathering ability.

Ed Lesesne was one of the first to volunteer in one of these missions and ended up on a night raid with some SEALs. They were to go along the Mekong, turn into a small tributary, then set up an ambush of a North Vietnamese group which was carrying payroll money for the Communist troops.

The ambush site was a bend in the small river. The SEALs were to be at the far end, while Lesesne and several Vietnamese were to be at the crook in the river. He was not to do anything until the SEALs fired first.

Later he told me about the mission. He said after two hours of waiting he saw several small canoes skimming over the water, barely visible in the dim light of a quarter moon. He trained his Stoner machine gun on them and waited . . . and waited. But nothing happened. Finally, he said, the nearest canoe was within ten yards of him. He felt he had no choice but to open fire. He pulled the trigger and knocked out the first canoe. Then the others in the group began firing. After it was all over, Lesesne said, he went to find out why there had been no initial fire from the Navy men. Then he laughed and threw his hands up into the air. "Those bastards had fallen asleep," he said.

As it was, the ambush killed the small party of North Vietnamese—plus it had robbed the Communist troops of their payday, something that always ruins the morale of soldiers. "There was money floating everywhere," Lesesne said.

IT WAS ONE of those rainy days when the downpour looked like spikes of silver aimed at the ground; a gloomy mist gathered over the land, creating a white curtain that partly obscured the distant hills. I sat on an ammo crate and puffed on a cigar, thinking about my 1962 visit to Laos. How had my people in the villages fared in the ensuing years. And what of Lani? What of the ten other babies I had helped deliver into this grim and heartless world?

Someday, I said to myself, I would return to Laos, to find the people I had known. I might even go back to the village where I had been held captive . . . back to the innocent people who had trusted me to return to them with medicine.

Christmas of 1968 passed by. My two sons were now nearly grown, and Lionel Jr., the eldest, was thinking of entering the Navy or the Coast Guard. I didn't try to tell him which one to enter, but I hinted in a letter that he might be better served not to be a foot soldier like his old man.

I wouldn't admit it to anyone, but going out on the missions and on patrols through the back country was starting to get me, just a little. I was now forty-five years old, weighed about 210 pounds, and while I could still run a fast mile or two without much strain, I began to feel aches and pains in my knees and arms. I knew the day would be coming when I would be summoned to headquarters and some kindly colonel would say something like, "Sergeant Pinn, you've done more than your share over here, maybe it's time to pull off the line and let some of the younger guys handle the fighting."

I didn't want somebody else telling me when that day came, or was about to come. That call should be made by me. One day in the spring of 1969 I went to Capt. Lesesne and asked if I could go on a mission again. It had been some time since I had been in the middle of a patrol and I wanted to go at least one more time before I had to pack it in.

Lesesne told me I was really needed at headquarters. Hell, I thought, he was sending himself on missions. So I did something I really didn't like—I went over my commanding officer's head. I walked over to 5th Special Forces headquarters and asked to see Col. Fred Abt, who was the commanding officer. Abt was out, but the executive officer of the 5th, Lt. Col. Clyde Sincere, was in his office and he agreed to see me.

"What can I do for you, First Sergeant Pinn?" he said.

I stood at attention. "Sir, I want to go on a mission with a team."

Sincere grinned up at me. "What kind of mission?"

"Anything, sir. I just want to go out. I've been sitting around here for weeks and weeks."

"You're needed here," he said.

"Yes, sir, but I can be needed out there, too, sir," I replied.

"Why, First Sergeant?" he pursued.

I didn't want to sound too corny, but I went ahead and said: "Because I want to hear that bugle blow one more time, sir."

It was the sort of thing George Patton would have said . . . or maybe George Custer.

Sincere stood up, looked me right in the eye and folded his

arms. "Sergeant Pinn, I understand what you're telling me. I'm against this, but if Captain Lesesne says it's okay with him, then it's okay with me."

I nodded and snapped a salute. "Thank you, sir."

But Sincere pointed a finger at me and said, "I don't want to hear any 'Prairie Fire' calls coming from you. You run into trouble and you're on your own."

"Don't worry, sir, there'll be no 'Prairie Fire' calls from me," I said.

Then I left the office and went back to Lesesne, who gave grudging approval. I prepared for my next mission, my last mission. The next order that came down the pipe would be mine. I cleaned the Tommy gun again, working the parts to make sure it was in good order. Then I waited.

It had been a long career and I had been to a lot of places and seen a lot of combat. Now, knowing that I was coming to the end of the road, I began to worry about how I would do. I sure did not want to get captured again. Four times would be far too many. And I didn't want to suffer some wound that would ruin me, and leave me an invalid the rest of my life.

Yet, at the same time, I was eager for action, something I was trained for. If it meant trying to capture an enemy officer, I was for it. If it meant simply killing Communists, I would do that. But it had to be for something, it had to be for some good.

It was a warm April morning, with a few high clouds in the distance; a gentle breeze managed to raise a restless red dust devil on the far end of the compound, beyond where the helicopters lay waiting. We had consumed a good breakfast: eggs and sausage, toast, plenty of black coffee.

Two nights before I had received the orders for the so-called

"Mike force" mission into southeastern Laos. We were to try to recover electronic devices that had been planted near the Ho Chi Minh Trail, devices which gave our listening posts information on how much traffic was moving on the trail and how heavy it was. We used this to coordinate B-52 raids on the area. Now, headquarters wanted some of them back lest they fall into North Vietnamese hands. The trail through Laos was the main line of supply for the North Vietnamese, who cut across the border to try to evade American bombers.

There were twelve of us, three Green Berets and a dozen Montagnard tribesmen with us on the mission. The Yards, as we called them, were an aloof band of Vietnamese highlanders who shunned contact with most of the other people in the nation. Of Chinese descent, they were taller than the average Vietnamese, and were renowned for their fighting prowess. Most of them were good men, fought like wildcats, and hated the Communists.

As I gathered my rucksack, ammo bandolier, and canteens, I couldn't help but remember the March 1968 mission when I got hit with the unexploded grenade. I hoped this operation would be a little smoother. It had to be, I thought. It would be my last—at least for a while.

We loaded into the Huey, made our final checks, then watched the green ground fall away. The sun poured in through the glass and we circled, then shot off to the west. I remembered Sincere's mild admonishment about there being no Prairie Fire distress calls.

In less than thirty minutes we were crossing the border. Scattered below were huts and small rice paddies. Some farmers stopped and gazed up at us; a few children waved, but most paid us no heed.

The pilot turned and gestured, meaning we were near the

landing zone, I craned to get a better look. It was a fairly clear meadow circled by small trees; beyond was a large field of tall elephant grass, some of it dry and brown.

Coming in on a chopper at a landing zone in hostile country is one of the most awe-inspiring and empty feelings a man can experience. You're pumped up, maybe a little scared, but too busy to do anything but focus on the issue at hand. Is the enemy down there about to open fire? Are they going to wait until you're on the ground before they start shooting? And I always had a fear of stepping off right onto a pungi stick, a sharpened piece of bamboo that inflicts a painful, disabling wound in the foot.

And then we were down, scrambling. Nobody had fired, but the helicopter's noise and descent was an invitation to anyone within five miles to hurry to this point, that we were here. We unloaded the gear, then hunched down and ran. Now the chopper lifted, the pilot gave us a salute, and then he was gone, melting over the horizon.

It's an emply feeling that settles over you in such a moment. You're alone in the jungle grass. There is no Howard Johnson here. America seems a million miles away. We hurriedly cut across the field toward the line of brush and small trees, looking for some concealment. I didn't like being in the open meadow.

We had gone about forty-five or fifty yards, half the length of a football field, when the gunfire started. At first it was one or two weapons, AK-47s, it sounded like, and then several more joined in. Bullets crackled around us like angry hornets.

It was almost like they knew where we'd be landing, I thought. The only thing we could do was spread out, go prone, and return the fire. The mission was blown, I figured. Within another minute or so, more Communist troops entered the skirmish, their weapons belching spurts of flame throughout the thick undergrowth and trees, where there was some protection. We were in the open field, with nothing but grass for cover, and it didn't do well as armor. Some of the Communist soldiers got close enough to throw grenades.

One of the Yards got hit in the arm, and I did a quick patch job. Then another was hit in the shoulder. We were in a lot of trouble. It was about to get worse.

At that moment I heard some of the Yards shouting in a near panic. I glanced toward the woods—a flicker of orange flame shot into the sky, topped by a swirling plume of white smoke. Fire! The Communists had set the grass on fire and the wind was moving it in our direction. It was hissing and crackling loudly as it danced toward us.

This was a real prairie fire situation. We fired, then slid backwards across the field, trying to get to an area where the grass wasn't so high, where it wouldn't feed the flames. The wall of fire was roaring toward us and I was starting to feel the heat. With the fire raging in front of us, and automatic fire all around from a circling enemy, not to mention being badly outnumbered, we issued the Prairie Fire call which was the last-ditch plea for help from anyone.

It went to 5th Special Forces headquarters at Kontum, where Lt. Col. Sincere heard it, then sent back the following message:

"Break contact with enemy. Resume mission."

It was an incredible response, but we were in such a dire situation there wasn't time to react. We kept firing and backing away. Actually, I would learn later, Sincere sent that reply as a joke, his brand of humor. At the time I didn't think it was very funny, not with wounded around me and the rest of us in danger of being killed, either by bullets or fire. As if the fire weren't enough of a problem, some of the Yards disappeared. Before long we were down to us three SF guys and two Yards, the rest having fled or been killed. We sent another Prairie Fire distress call.

But by then the CCC at Kontum had passed the word to get help and before long some Air Force jets came screaming in and placed napalm bombs in the thick brush where the North Vietnamese were sheltered. The display was awesome, a sight that I never could quite take as routine. There was a THOOMP sound and an orgasm of fire billowed across the horizon. If I allowed myself to anguish over the horror that the enemy troops endured I would go crazy. The heat was so intense that we could feel the wave of energy sweep over our heads as we cowered in the dirt. I never saw napalm used that I didn't think about the Chinese kid in Korea, his skin fried.

Now, the gunfire was suppressed and we hurriedly gathered our wounded and rushed back toward the LZ. The surviving North Vietnamese, those who had fled the area before the napalm strike, anticipated our move, and were there waiting. I had a Yard over my shoulder and heard a loud smacking sound—followed almost instantly by the report of a rifle—and felt the wounded guy's body quiver with the impact of the bullet in his side. He groaned, and I shouted something dirty and fell down, easing the guy off and struggling for my weapon. There was blood on my clothing and on my weapon. I fired a long burst, stopped and chucked my last grenade. We were in it again. But at the last moment the jets came screaming in, this time ripping the jungle with half dozen .50 caliber machine guns. The din was unbelievable, with bark and leaves flying in all directions.

After they had roared into the blue, there was no more firing, and we heard cries and moans coming from the enemy. Moments later, I saw the Huey coming in, the pop-pop-pop sound music to our ears. We stood up and cheered, then began moving as rapidly as we could to the grassy area in the center of the field.

All of us had been wounded. When we got back, Capt. Lesesne was there waiting, telling me that I was not to go on any more missions, that he needed help at company headquarters.

26

The World from House 10

NOT LONG AFTER the mission, the Army presented me with another Purple Heart, my eighth. I remember the first one back in 1944. Lesesne asked me about it.

"I sent it home to my mother," I said. "Like most mothers, she was proud of her son. So she showed the Purple Heart to some of the ladies in the neighborhood. One of them said, 'It's so pretty. Do you think he could get one for me?' That's a true story, sir."

Not long after that Lesesne left, and then I left. My replacement was M/Sgt. Robert Howard, who had received the Medal of Honor in Vietnam. What a great guy he was, probably the most decorated soldier in Vietnam. There were a lot of good men there. But it was frustrating for me. The war in Vietnam, and the war in Korea, too, were jokes. Ugly jokes, but jokes just the same. We didn't win in either of them, not because we couldn't win, but because it was a political operation more than a military one. The leadership failed us, especially in Vietnam. If we had made a real effort to win, we could have. We started off there with about 440 men—mostly Green Berets—and we were doing a pretty good job. Then the politicians started sending more troops there. Soon there were 500,000 Americans there, so many that they were getting in each other's way. There were too many to do the job. I saw the morale of our troops begin to fall right after the Tet offensive in February, 1968. They started smoking all kinds of junk and just going to hell in a hand basket.

I personally never gave up believing that we had a rightful place to help Vietnam maintain its freedom from the Communists. I still believe in it. I believe we could have won.

But my fighting was over after that last mission in 1969. The Green Berets transferred me out of Kontum and sent me to Saigon, which was relatively safe. I was put in charge of House Number 10, a two-story structure which was called a "safe house," a place where the Special Forces guys on rest and relaxation could spend a few days taking life easy. There was a bar in the place, plus several bedrooms. We hired some big Chinese men to be the guards, and they would not allow anyone in without ID and orders. I told the guys who came there that it was strictly for rest. "If you want to get laid," I said, "go to another part of town."

I personally enjoyed sitting at the bar, sipping good whiskey, and watching TV. But the news broadcasts from the U.S. soon began to bother me a little, then a lot. It angered me to see the anti-war demonstrations back home. Long-haired boys with flowers in their hair. Everyone was out in the streets shooting off their mouths about soldiers in Vietnam. The behavior of these young people made my blood boil. They had lost their sense of decency.

College kids. . . . I got my education out in the woods, working with the CCC in the late 1930's. It was some of the best training and the best experience a young fellow could have. When I went into the Army, at my father's insistence, I at first tried to get into the Army Air Corps. But I didn't do well on my eye exam. So afterwards these three officers sat me down at a table and asked why I wanted to be a flier. I told them it looked exciting. Then they asked about my education.

I told them, "I went to Harvard and I went to M.I.T."

One of them, his voice tinged with disbelief, said, "You went to Harvard and M.I.T.? How did you do that?"

I shrugged. "I went in the front door and out the back."

"Get out of here," the officer said.

PART FOUR

RETREAT

27

Retirement and Judy

I RETIRED FROM the Army in 1970 and drifted about, taking several jobs, most of them in the tourist industry. I spent some time in Las Vegas as a police officer. Then I obtained a job at a motel in Guntersville, Alabama, a town of about 10,000 situated on a beautiful lake formed when the TVA built dams on the Tennessee River.

I met a girl named Judy McCoy who worked at the same place, and even though I was more than twenty years older, we fell in love and one day I asked her to marry me.

At the time I was attached to the 20th Special Forces of the Army National Guard. The unit headquarters was in Birmingham, but I was placed on duty as an advisor in Huntsville. As it turned out, my sergeant-in-charge was old Albert Slugocki. Judy and I were going to be married in her hometown, Guntersville, and I asked Albert to be the best man. A lot of the guests came to the event and some of them started drinking before the ceremony. Anyway, the minister had some sort of speech impairment, and when the part came for us to exchange the rings, the minister said to Albert, "The ring, please."

Well, Albert had a hearing impairment, courtesy of the wars in Korea and Vietnam, plus his reactions were a little blurred by the whiskey.

So the preacher repeated, "Give me the ring, please."

Albert looked at him and said, "What was that?"

Somebody in the audience, obviously half drunk, blurted loudly, "Give him the fucking ring."

Actually I wasn't sure what was said, but I knew there was sort of a stir, and I saw a look of surprise flash across Albert's face and he dug into his pocket and produced the ring. I placed it on Judy's finger. After the ceremony, I heard a stir and heard Sgt. Marty Duran talking loudly with Albert.

"You screwed up his wedding and he's mad as hell," Duran was saying.

Someone else said, "I think Lionel's looking for his .45."

With that, Duran and Albert moved out, and I was told later that Duran drove him home. I never got mad about anything. I was happy to be married. I saw Albert a few days later and he apologized for anything that may have happened.

"Well, it wasn't your fault that somebody in the audience used some bad language," I said.

Albert nodded. Then, referring to the preacher, he said, "I couldn't hear the fucker."

Our marriage blessed us with one child, a dark-haired beauty we named Wenonah. She was born in 1973. At the time I was still a Catholic, though not a good one. But I wanted her baptized and the church requires that there be a godfather and godmother. Judy found someone to be the godmother and it was my job to find the godfather.

An old friend of the family, Gen. William Rosson, came to mind. Rosson and I had served together in Special Forces at McDill AFB, Florida, in 1964 and later in Vietnam. He was a Green Beret advisor at one time; later he became Gen. William Westmoreland's chief of staff. Anyway, Rosson was in the Canal

Zone, commander-in-chief of the Southern Command.

I called him and after some switching about, I got him. I told him I wanted him to be the godfather, if he could arrange to be off duty for a day or two.

"I'd be honored," he said. "But I can't get loose right now."

We decided he could be the godfather by proxy, so to speak. And that's how we did it. Wenonah grew up never seeing the man who was her godfather, but she did send Rosson a picture on occasion.

LIKE A LOT of retired military guys, I worried about where this country was headed in the years following Vietnam. Everytime I turned around it seemed we heard a news story from the war, about how the higher ups had lied to the soldiers and the people of the nation. I had some doubts that we could hold our own if we got into an all-war with the Soviet Union. Ever since World War II we had gone down hill. We won the big one, but were tied in Korea. Now we had been beaten in Vietnam.

I was fretting about this one day when I received a telephone call at my home in Guntersville.

"Hey, you crazy Indian, you're still alive." a husky voice said.

It took just a second for my brain to register the familiar accent.

"Ed Leeming!" I shouted. "You're still alive. Where are you now?"

"I'm here in Guntersville," he said. "I saw your name in the bulletin about a reunion and decided to give you a call."

"The hell you say," I cried, in my best retired-sergeant voice.

He laughed. "Yeah, when I saw your name and phone number

I knew I had to come see you. I told my wife we were taking a trip. I brought her with me."

I gave directions and a few minutes later they were there at the house. In this world, there are old friends and dear friends. But there is no closer bond than between those who have shared combat together.

When Leeming came up the walk I went out to meet him and we embraced.

A flood of memories welled up inside and we both blinked hard to keep back the tears.

"We've grown a little older," he said.

"And damned lucky to do so," I said. "God, Ed, we left a lot of good men over there. Boys. Just boys, most of them."

"I never thought we'd see each other again," Leeming said, his voice halting. "I didn't know if we'd ever get out of that place."

Some of the others had made it out, but had since died, he said. One of them was our platoon leader, Ben Gibbons.

"He was a fine man," I said. "He was a leader, even though he was fairly young."

Leeming sat down on the porch then, nodding. But he said nothing.

I knew the two of them had had their differences in Korea, for some reason.

"You two ever talk?" I asked.

He nodded again. "A few years ago. It was OK."

"Good." Then I laughed. "I guess you and me are about the last two old S.O.B.s from the original platoon."

"I guess we are," he said. "From the group that went over in '50."

"You know what I remember most about Gibbons?" I asked. "He was always so serious. I never saw him smile."

Ed shook his head slightly. "I guess there wasn't a whole lot to smile about in Korea."

"There wasn't," I said. "It was the forgotten war."

28

Action in Grenada

CIVILIAN LIFE WAS OK, but I often yearned for action. The chance came in October 1983 when President Reagan decided to invade the island of Grenada. I learned about it when I got a call from Robert K. Brown, publisher of Soldier of Fortune magazine. He was chartering a plane to fly out to the Caribbean island and see what was about to happen. I was packed and ready to go in thirty minutes, rushed to Birmingham to catch a plane to link up with him in Florida. Also making the trip were writer Jim Graves and reporter Jay Mallin of the Washington Times.

The reason (we learned later) that America struck the island was because it appeared to be a buildup site for the Soviet Union and Cuba, a place that would become an island fortress. Secondly, and perhaps more importantly, there were American students who were being harassed by Cuban soldiers and who faced the prospect of being captured—or worse. Thirdly, the prime minister, Maurice Bishop, whom the U.S. supported, had been assassinated after being captured at his spacious hilltop palace as he played basketball. A revolutionary government led by Gen. Hudson Austin and Deputy Prime Minister Bernard Coard had taken over.

We winged across the gray, placid waters of the North Atlantic, which gradually gave way to the sparkling green-blue of the Caribbean. Within a few hours we saw the point of siege. The invasion, a probable victory for America after the long nightmare of Vietnam, had already begun. We saw smoky trails of rocket fire arcing toward the lush green hillsides. Just as we nosed in for a landing, we observed an American AC-130 Specter unleashing a spurt of 40mm cannon rounds at the Butler House, the home of the assassinated prime minister. It was now occupied by the enemy, and they were literally catching hell: the place was burning in a fury at rooftop.

We recognized the house and it didn't take long for us to surmise that there were some things inside worth salvaging . . . maybe even gold. We saw a group of American paratroopers moving in a crouch, running by the parked planes. We unloaded rapidly, grabbed what gear we could carry, and rushed outside. It wasn't at all like Vietnam, but there was some shooting going on. We laid low for much of the day until the firing diminished. Now, more U.S. troops were onshore, moving in files toward a strong point which was defended by Cuban troops.

While this was an invasion, it was not an all-out war. Some parts of the island seemed to be quite peaceful. A group of American students were sheltered at a motel. Brown and I figured it was best to get a place to stay, then try to get back to the palace later that night.

We obtained rooms at the St. James Hotel, ate supper, had a drink, then ventured out into the warm Caribbean night. There were American troops guarding key points, but we were not challenged since we were members of the press. We moved hurriedly and were soon at the fire-damaged Butler House. The place was quiet, no movement anywhere, just some smoke swirling into the night.

"They don't have the place guarded," Brown said.

I was dumbfounded. This was the home of the prime minister. There had to be documents in there that the Reagan administration could find valuable. But apparently, the commanders felt the place was secure and no one would tamper with it.

We scrambled the last fifty feet and entered the front door. To our amazement, a big safe lay on the floor, almost buried in a pile of rubble. The thing had crashed down through two floors, taking out ceilings, chandeliers, and rafters. The damn thing was just laying there for the taking, smoldering from the fire. It was plenty hot. Brown ventured that it probably contained gold as well as other valuables.

We moved about in the darkness, but couldn't see well enough to get at the lock. I suggested the best way was to blow it. But we didn't have any equipment, and none of us wanted to find enough large shells to construct a bomb. We decided to wait until morning. It would cool off by then.

When we came back at daybreak, the house was still unguarded. Meanwhile, I had found an acetylene torch and began burning away the lock. The door came open finally and I looked inside and could see currency, big bundles of it.

I turned to my companions. "Enough money in here to buy off Castro's whole army." The others laughed.

But then the laughter stopped. As I reached in the money turned out to be a mess of burned paper . . . only the ends were intact. The rest had been so badly singed as to be unusable. Personally, I had hoped Brown was right about gold. But there was none. Yet we didn't come away empty-handed. In the safe and in other parts of the house, we found documents that showed Cuba and the Soviet Union intended to make the island a Communist stronghold. There were also shipping papers for thousands of rifles and small arms, far more than this small nation could ever use.

And finally, I came away with the basketball Prime Minister Bishop had been using when the revolutionaries captured him.

I left the press people for an hour or so and went to visit with the troops. I saw a couple of paratroopers sitting on a dune overlooking the beach.

"How are we doing?" I asked.

"OK," one of them said. "A little tired."

I nodded. Then I asked, "What would you like right now if you could get it?"

The answer, I figured, would be something like a frosty beer or a cold Coca-Cola. Instead, one of them replied, "A letter from home."

I didn't say anything, just nodded at him. I know that any time a young man is being shot at, it's a big war. But Grenada was a breeze compared to New Guinea, Korea, or Vietnam. A letter from home? My God, I thought, these guys had only been gone a couple of days.

29

Return to Laos

ONE NIGHT I dreamed about Laos, a mish-mash of events that made me wake up in a sweat. My ancestors put a lot of faith in dreams, and while I liked to cling to my heritage, I viewed life more realistically. But the dream about Laos was about some of the babies I had helped deliver. In the dream they were grown people and they were calling me to come to them. Then somebody would start shooting them and they would fall screaming. I had the dream several times over the years; it would always wake me up. I would have to sit up and light a cigar.

But in 1987 I finally decided I might have to go back to Laos and see what was going on over there. Maybe the dream meant nothing. But again, I reasoned, maybe there is some ancient spirit that harkens to us in our sleep.

On a more realistic note, I had always figured on one day going back over there to see some of the people in the villages where I had been a river doctor. I had promised them that I would come back. Now, in 1987, a quarter-century had passed. Those babies—if they hadn't been executed—would be grown. Maybe I would meet some of them, or perhaps once again see the mothers.

I told my wife I was shipping out for the Orient, and she

didn't believe me at first. But I used my credit cards to the maximum and purchased a round-trip ticket, and also bought some medical supplies, such as aspirin, Tylenol, and bandages. I would not go there empty-handed. But the main reason I was going was that I believed that I might find some of the Americans who were still listed as missing in action. Some of them were undoubtedly in Laos.

Finally, there was the spiritual awakening that I had slowly undergone since leaving the military, and awareness that brought me closer not only to the Great Spirit, or God, if you will, but also to my heritage as an American Indian. I had spent much of my time studying the history of both the Micmac and the Osage, my ancestors. My mother and father had always honored their forebears by taking part in the ancient ceremonies, and both had the traditional attire of our people. I inherited my father's deerskin tunic and leggings, plus the head-dress of eagle and hawk feathers. I carried them through the airport at Atlanta, catching a lot of stares as I waited to board the plane. It became a conversation piece in flight, and I relayed the story of my family to a number of fellow travelers. It passed the time as we cruised over the Pacific. Then I slept, remembering other flights to Asia. Those had not been so easy-going, so peaceful. But my return to Laos would be anything but a tranquil visit.

We stopped over for several hours in Bangkok, Thailand, where security guards went through my things and asked the purpose of my trip. Then I boarded another flight and soon I was looking down on the misty green fields and awesome mountains that soared like thunder gods above the river valleys.

Then, we approached the airport at Saraboury, and I watched eagerly as the ground began to rise toward us. For a moment I glanced into the window at my own reflection. Once before, I had come here as a muscular young soldier. Now, the face that looked back at me was a lined, wrinkled countenance, fringed with slightly graying hair. I was sixty-four. But what the hell, I was still a warrior at heart. I quickly eased into the fringed tunic, and placed the head-dress over the gray hair.

As I alighted I heard some excited jabbering and saw a police officer pointing at me, obviously alarmed at the sight of an American Indian coming down the ramp. Another officer appeared and spoke in stilted English, "You come with us, please."

They ushered me into a small room adjoining the passenger waiting area. There were two chairs in the room, a small fan on a table. The walls were painted green and were bare. They told me to sit in one of the chairs. For an hour or so I sat in silence, trying to appear casual and unruffled. Then two Lao soldiers entered the room, AK-47 rifles held at port arms. They were followed by a slender man in a loose-fitting blue suit, with padded shoulders that appeared much too large. He wore silver-framed glasses and was smoking a cigarette. He bowed slightly, then sat down, fixing a cold stare on me.

"Who are you?" he asked. "Why have you come here?"

I told him my name. "I'm an American Indian. I've come in peace. In 1962 I came to know some of the people in the villages along the Mekong. I wanted to go back and see them, take them some medicine."

He took a deep draw on the cigarette and continued to study me. Then: "Why have you come here?" I repeated my answer. But the man shook his head. "Who asked you to come here? Did anyone ask you to come? You are not welcome here."

I shrugged. "I was welcome when I helped the people of the villages long ago. I think they would welcome me."

After a time the man gestured to the guards and one of them

left the room, then returned shortly with a glass of water. They offered it to me. I shook my head. The man in the suit picked it up, drank it, then resumed his questioning. The tone of his voice went from puzzlement to exasperation.

I told him again my name and why I had come, to visit the people in the villages and show America's friendship. Finally the man left, leaving me with the two sullen-faced guards, who kept their weapons leveled at me. I thought I stood a chance of being killed. Maybe it hadn't been such a good idea to come here, I thought. Surely, if they were going to shoot me, they'd take me out and do it, they just wouldn't blow me away in a room at the airport.

For a long time we sat there in silence. I asked for a drink of water, gesturing as though I held an invisible glass. One of the guards left and came back with water. I asked to go to the restroom, and both of them followed me, standing a few feet away while I urinated. Then we returned to the room. For the rest of the day we stayed there, saying nothing. As night came, one of them pulled up the second chair and slumped in it, leaning his weapon against the wall beside him. The other slid to the floor, wearily wiping a hand across his eyes. He, too, put his weapon against the wall. I sat saying nothing, my eyes on the weapons. In another hour, both men had dozed off.

I glanced about to make sure there were no cameras in the room. There were no windows. No one could see in. I quickly reached out and quietly took the nearest weapon, carefully easing it to me. I was afraid of leaning too far, lest the chair squeak. Then, slowly I pushed the release button and eased the magazine out.

Then I gingerly removed the top shell from the magazine and turned it around. I reinserted the magazine, and slowly bent back and put the weapon against the wall. Neither man had roused from his slumber. They seemed to be knocked out. I stood up, quickly grabbed the second weapon, and turned around the top bullet in the magazine.

Then I sat down and waited. Now, if they attempted to shoot me, the weapons would not fire, and I would stand a chance of jumping them. However, before anything so drastic took place, the guards stirred, then woke up. And none too soon either. By now the sun had come up and the man in the suit returned. He gestured for me to follow him, telling me to leave my baggage there. I didn't like the sound of it. But I showed no emotion. The man spoke to the guards, and they stoically gathered up their weapons and left. I breathed a little easier. At least I wouldn't have those Soviet-made rifles staring down my throat. The man drove me to a small building near the airport.

There, a second man sat behind a desk in a small office, nervously smoking a cigarette. He told me he was a representative of the local government, and was instructed to assist me in returning to America.

I shrugged. "I can get on the plane by myself if you want me to leave. But I had hoped to visit with some of the villages."

The man nodded, puffed on the cigarette, then motioned for the other man to come with him outside. They left me in the office for several minutes, then returned. The government official then asked me some of the same qustions I had been asked before. Then he said, "We will ask that you go peacefully back onto the plane and return to where you came from. We will not accept you here. Your visit is not permitted."

I was then driven back to the airport by the first man who had questioned me. My attempt to visit the villages, to look for MIAs, had ended. It was a failure. But at least I tried. I did take note of the city, which had changed considerably in twenty-five years. The streets were clean as before and there were still the vendors and the little markets. But everyone, it seemed, was riding around on a motor scooter or motor bike.

And then something caught my attention, that set off a red alarm. Along the outskirts of the city I caught a glimpse of a Caucasian man who appeared to be supervising workers in erecting power lines.

"Who's the guy?" I asked.

"I cannot say," my tour guide replied.

Cannot? I wondered. Or will not.

"He live alone here?" I pursued.

He smiled. "He has a wife. Very beautiful wife. Lucky man."

They guy might have been a Russian or a Czech. But somehow I doubted it. I think he was an American who got caught up in a hopeless situation and decided after a time to just make the best of it. I looked at some of the pretty woman walking lithely along the street; they were all slim and vivacious. Maybe you couldn't blame a man for staying . . .

The Lao soldiers and police escorted me back to a plane and I made the return flight back to America. Coming home, I found no one from the State Department waiting, nor anyone from the military. No one seemed interested in my trip, and few questioned me about the man I had seen. There was a lot of interest from the credit card companies. They wanted to be paid. I had maxed out all my cards and ruined what credit I had.

30

Old Soldiers, All

THE SPECIAL FORCES vets held reunions regularly and for a long time I attended. Some of my old friends were often there, people like Clyde Sincere, Jack Abraham, and so many others. Sometimes, though, things got a little wacky, or rather, I enjoyed a few too many glasses of bourbon. Or maybe just too many good Mexican cigars.

One year, in the late 1980s, there was a raffle to be held at the end of the final day of our meeting. We were in Las Vegas, in one of those big banquet rooms that is separated by a sliding divider panel. We were to have the place until 5:30. In the adjoining section, a wedding party was coming in for a reception at that time.

Anyway, the raffle was held and lo, and behold, I was proclaimed the winner. I was feeling pretty good. And I heard Clyde or someone calling, "Come on up here, Lionel, and get your prize."

The prize was a big shotgun. Well, at the same time people were telling me to go up there. I heard raucous sounds coming from the other side of the banquet hall.

Somebody says, "That doggone wedding group is here already. And it's only 4:30."

They were not only there, but they were playing music loudly and you could hear shouts and laughter.

"That's too damn loud," I called out. "They shouldn't be there yet."

"Go get your shotgun, Lionel," someone shouted, slapping me on the shoulder.

They meant for me to collect my prize. I misread the words, thinking they wanted me to get my gun and take some action. By now I got up to the stage and went to the podium where the master of ceremonies handed me the weapon. The group cheered and applauded. But my attention was on the wedding next door. I called to Sincere, "Why are those people here already?"

Clyde sort of shrugged and grinned, like it was no big deal (which it wasn't).

But I was in a roaring good mood. I held up the shotgun and shouted, "I'll put a stop to their racket."

Someone called, "Hold on, Lionel. It's OK. It's just a wedding."

I raised the shotgun aloft and said, "They're not supposed to be there yet. I'll fix them."

And then I lowered the weapon and held it like it had a fixed bayonet, and began charging toward the wedding party.

Fortunately, I tripped, and went sprawling on the carpeted floor, as a roar of laughter went up.

"Thank God," one of the men called.

By then I was surrounded by comrades who had cooler heads and better judgment. They steered me back to our area of the ballroom and the evening ended in jolly good fun. I'm glad I never made it to the wedding party.

One evening I stopped by a bar for a glass of good bourbon on the rocks. A pretty young waitress came to take my order. She returned a few moments later just as I had opened a big Mexican cigar. She watched warily as I fumbled for a lighter.

"Are you planning to light that thing?" she asked.

I glanced up at her. "I had figured on it."

In a low but icy voice she declared, "You do and it's going out of here and you're going with it. Do you read me?"

"Yes, ma'am," I said quickly, taking the cigar from my mouth. "I'll have my drink and be on my way."

And I was. I've been beaten by men in fights before, but I wasn't going to let a pretty girl kick my behind. And that girl looked mad enough to do it.

For a veteran of combat, the war is never far away . . . even when fifty years have gone by there are the dreams that come in your sleep or when you're doing something as simple as having coffee in the morning. Suddenly, it's there . . . flashes and eerie black-and-white images. When I think of Korea, I see Ed Leeming, Lt. Gibbons, Johnny Coyle and the others of the 2nd Infantry Division. The images of World War II sometimes drift farther on the horizon. But they're there. Once I went out back just to feed a stray dog and as I watched it eat, a ghostly picture appeared and I heard the sounds of the machine gun firing that day Lt. Chasteen was killed in the Philippines.

But my most vivid memories of war would be Vietnam. That's where the Green Berets were, and they were the best soldiers ever. Men like Frank Taylor, Robert Howard, Ed Lesesne, Roy Bahr, Lee Mize, Jim Morris, and Clyde Sincere and so many others occupy a place in my heart, my brain, my very soul. I see them often.

I never liked to identify myself with the so-called "common soldiers," such as those who were in the regular Army units. They didn't possess the skills nor the desire to be great soldiers like the Green Berets.

At heart, I knew I would always be a soldier. In 1983 when they put up the Vietnam War Memorial I wondered whether I wanted to go there. It wasn't that I couldn't go, or that, as Jane Fonda and some others might say, I should go with a "support group." I didn't need a support group. I just didn't think I wanted to go. I lost friends in Vietnam, but their deaths were no more bitter than the guys who died in the frozen hell of Korea, or in the sweltering heat of New Guinea.

"Aw, hell," I said to myself. "I'm not going there."

But I drove to Washington and said I was going for the purpose of visiting Arlington, the graves of my father and my old short-term friend, Ira Hayes. It was a cold, rainy October afternoon, the drizzle swirling around the red and orange autumn leaves. They would be gone soon, the leaves. In this kind of weather, they didn't drift to the ground, they were wrenched from the branches violently, suddenly . . . like the young soldiers who died in war.

As I stood there I suddenly thought of those kids in the 4th Division, the ones who were screaming as the helicopter was consumed by flames and then the reddish-orange burst as the fuel went up . . . how there wasn't a two-inch piece of flesh left to identify those who perished . . . young men who, just seconds before, were ordinary American boys who wanted nothing more than to live out their lives.

And so on that grim and gray October 1987 I went to the Vietnam Wall. I needed to see the Wall. It was more than a case of wanting to see it. I had to do it. As I drew near, it was as though I could hear the voices of those I'd known years before.

There it was before me, sloping off into the mist, which hung over the place like a band of ghosts. There was a crowd there, standing five or six deep, all along the thing, squinting in the rain for a glimpse of a name. A guy in a suit and tie and Ivy League trench coat was in front of me. He turned and our eyes locked.

For a moment we said nothing, then he smiled slightly and nodded several times. I nodded back. He had been there, I could tell. And he knew I'd been there. We didn't have to explain it. Without a word, he reached out and we shook hands. Then he moved on. He must have been one of the young soldiers, the young common soldiers who had fought.

I touched it, then put my hands on it, both of them, for a minute or so, leaning slightly, aware now that my eyes were watering badly. "Pinn, you were always a sensitive S.O.B.," I whispered to myself, blinking hard. Then I backed away and knelt down on one knee, reached into my pocket and pulled out the Combat Infantryman Badge, the one with the two silver service stars. I placed it on the ground, with the back leaning on the Wall. And then I got up and went back a few steps.

They were common soldiers, most of them . . . but what they did there made them quite uncommon. I stood looking at the Wall and for a moment I saw the bleak, frozen hills of Korea . . . and I saw the rolling green fields of Gettysburg, and it became clear to me then. "They're all the same," I said to myself.

And they were. The common and the uncommon . . . the heroes and those who simply were there, who died cringing and flinching and crying for their mothers.

Now they belonged to the ages. They were one. And they are the nobility.

After-Battle Report

In March of 1997, Lionel Pinn was diagnosed with leukemia. Doctors felt it was caused by exposure to radiation, a result of the 1953 atomic bomb tests. He was taken to University Hospital in Birmingham, Alabama. Always the optimist, he bantered with doctors after getting the stunning news.

"Hell, I've been in tougher fights than this." Then, later: "Why, hell, I always thought I'd die of old age." At the time he was seventy-four.

But as it would turn out, Pinn was in his toughest battle. One night, he tossed and turned in his hospital bed, and at one point called out, "The white blood cells are attacking the red ones and the whites one are beating the hell out of the red ones. I'm hurting worse than I ever did in all those wars."

Pinn and I began working on this book sometime in late 1995 and had just started to really get some serious interviewing done when he began to feel sick from time to time. None of us knew how serious it was, at first. Later, some of the interviewing was done in the hospital room, times when he was undergoing chemotherapy. He was not in the best frame of mind, and his memory failed him from time to time. He did not always remember names of comrades.

And sometimes he just did not want to use names.

Some of his stories are almost beyond belief. Yet, men who knew him in Korea or Vietnam say that Pinn was the type of soldier who did incredible things. He had a spirit to him, they said, that would not allow him to ever give up or quit.

His struggle with leukemia showed that side of him. In 1997, when he entered the hospital, a doctor told him he would be lucky to be alive for a year.

But, by year's end, the prognosis had changed. One of them said the leukemia was in remission. "He might beat this thing," a hospital spokesman said.

Over the coming months he was in and out of the hospital. Then, in November 1998, his daughter, Wenonah, then twenty-five, was to be married to Mike Resha. But Pinn was back in the hospital, and so weak he had difficulty getting out of bed.

"I'm not going to miss her wedding," he said. "I've looked forward to this day for years. She's my only daughter. I'm walking her down the aisle."

Doctors said otherwise. Said one, "Your life is more important than a wedding."

Finally, Pinn relented, saying he'd asked an old friend to be a stand-in. The old friend was retired Gen. William B. Rosson, the chief of staff to Gen. William Westmoreland in Vietnam.

On November 7, 1998, Rosson was at Victory Baptist Church in Guntersville, tuxedo in hand, just in case he was needed. Not only were he and Pinn friends, he said, but he had at last met the girl who was his goddaughter, Wenonah Pinn.

"She's even more beautiful than I had imagined," he said. "She makes a radiant bride."

But the General was not needed. Pinn talked the doctors into letting him out of the hospital, and he escorted his lovely, dark-haired daughter down the aisle. The old soldier lost his balance once, but quickly recovered.

Pinn continued his delaying battle against leukemia. Even in declining health the spirit of the warrior burned inside him. He volunteered to work with the Alabama Committee for Employer Support of the Guard and Reserve. In that post, he often went to Fort Benning, Georgia, to help process troops being sent to Bosnia and later Kosovo. One day as the troops were leaving, Pinn fell in line and boarded the plane.

When it landed in Germany, an Army officer thanked him for his loyalty, but said he had to go back to America.

An old friend and fellow Green Beret, Fred Fine, explained, "He just wanted to go over there and help out. Lionel just wanted to be where the action was."

On August 7, 1999, Lionel Pinn died. He was seventy-six. There was a Catholic service for him at Carr Funeral Home in Guntersville. A young man sang the song Pinn had requested for his final service—"Ballad of the Green Berets."

He was buried at Arlington National Cemetery. And there he will forever hear the bugles calling . . .

www.ingramcontent.com/pod-product-compliance
Lightning Source LLC
Chambersburg PA
CBHW022059160426
43198CB00008B/283